Presented to

....

From

....

Date

....

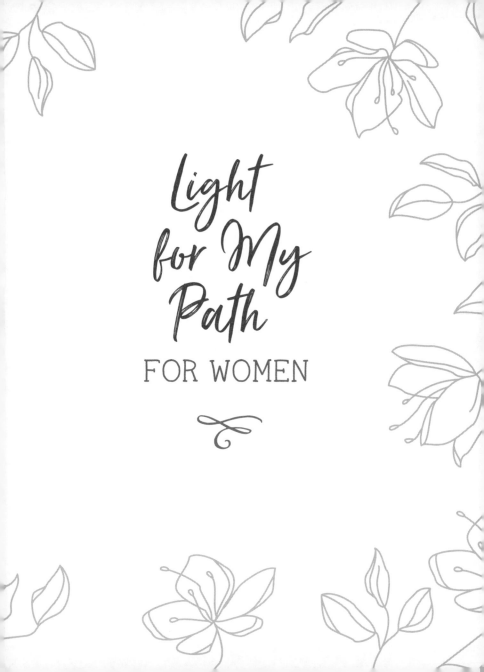

Light
for My
Path

FOR WOMEN

Light for My Path

FOR WOMEN

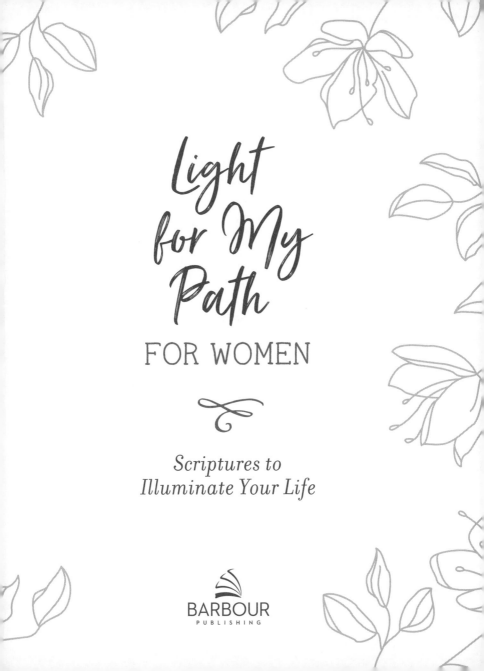

Scriptures to Illuminate Your Life

BARBOUR
PUBLISHING

© 2008 by Barbour Publishing, Inc.

ISBN 978-1-64352-885-4

Published by Barbour Publishing Inc., 1810 Barbour Drive, Uhrichsville, Ohio 44683, www.barbourbooks.com

Our mission is to inspire the world with the life-changing message of the Bible.

Member of the
Evangelical Christian
Publishers Association

Printed in China.

Contents

Introduction

Our world sends many conflicting signals on the important issues of life. How should we approach adversity? Why speak with honesty? Is prayer for real? What is true wisdom?

In His kindness, God has answered all of these questions—and many more—in the pages of His Word, the Bible. Whatever our needs, we can find in scripture the principles we need to address the issues we face.

Light for My Path for Women is a collection of Bible verses relating to many important questions of life. In these pages, you'll find carefully selected scriptures that address topics like comfort, encouragement, friendship, mercy, rest, and understanding. In fact, nearly four dozen categories are covered, arranged alphabetically for ease of use.

This book is not intended to replace regular, personal Bible study. It is simply a quick reference to some of the key issues of life that women most often face. We hope it will be an encouragement to you as you read.

Adversity

If our lives are easy, and if all we ever attempt for God is what we know we can handle, how will we ever experience His omnipotence in our lives?
ANNE GRAHAM LOTZ

Beloved, think it not strange concerning the fiery trial which is to try you, as though some strange thing happened unto you: But rejoice, inasmuch as ye are partakers of Christ's sufferings; that, when his glory shall be revealed, ye may be glad also with exceeding joy.
1 PETER 4:12–13 KJV

"Blessed are you when people hate you, when they exclude you and insult you and reject your name as evil, because of the Son of Man."
LUKE 6:22 NIV

In his kindness God called you to share in his eternal glory by means of Christ Jesus. So after you have suffered a little while, he will restore, support, and strengthen you, and he will place you on a firm foundation.
1 PETER 5:10 NLT

As we have suffered much for Christ and have shared in
His pain, we also share His great comfort. But if we are
in trouble, it is for your good. And it is so you will be saved
from the punishment of sin. If God comforts us, it is for your
good also. You too will be given strength not to give up
when you have the same kind of trouble we have.

2 CORINTHIANS 1:5–6 NLV

For I reckon that the sufferings of this present time
are not worthy to be compared with the glory
which shall be revealed in us.

ROMANS 8:18 KJV

For our light and momentary troubles are achieving
for us an eternal glory that far outweighs them all.

2 CORINTHIANS 4:17 NIV

If we endure hardship, we will reign with him.

2 TIMOTHY 2:12 NLT

If men speak bad of you because you are a
Christian, you will be happy because the Spirit
of shining-greatness and of God is in you.

1 PETER 4:14 NLV

Is anyone among you in trouble? Let them pray.

JAMES 5:13 NIV

That the trial of your faith, being much more precious
than of gold that perisheth, though it be tried with fire,
might be found unto praise and honour and glory
at the appearing of Jesus Christ.
1 PETER 1:7 KJV

The LORD hears his people when they call to him
for help. He rescues them from all their troubles.
PSALM 34:17 NLT

"I have told you these things so you may have
peace in Me. In the world you will have much trouble.
But take hope! I have power over the world!"
JOHN 16:33 NLV

Yea, and all that will live godly in
Christ Jesus shall suffer persecution.
2 TIMOTHY 3:12 KJV

*Heavenly Father, I feel the darkness encompassing me.
The burden is so heavy to bear. I thank You that You have
promised to take this weight from me. I will surrender
it to You, leaving it in Your loving hands. Amen.*

Comfort

You do not need to continue dealing with your own burdens and sorrows and grief. You may turn them over to Jesus, who stands ready to receive them. It is His will to comfort and heal all who come to Him in faith.

RUBYE GOODLETT

And God shall wipe away all tears from their eyes;
and there shall be no more death, neither sorrow,
nor crying, neither shall there be any more pain:
for the former things are passed away.

REVELATION 21:4 KJV

And I will pray the Father, and he shall give you another
Comforter, that he may abide with you for ever.

JOHN 14:16 KJV

"And I am with you always, even to the end of the world."

MATTHEW 28:20 NLV

"As a mother comforts her child,
so will I comfort you."

ISAIAH 66:13 NIV

Be joyful. Grow to maturity. Encourage each other.
Live in harmony and peace. Then the God of
love and peace will be with you.
2 Corinthians 13:11 nlt

Blessed are they that mourn: for they shall be comforted.
Matthew 5:4 kjv

Praise be to the God and Father of our Lord Jesus Christ,
the Father of compassion and the God of all comfort,
who comforts us in all our troubles, so that we can comfort
those in any trouble with the comfort we ourselves receive
from God. For just as we share abundantly in the sufferings
of Christ, so also our comfort abounds through Christ.
2 Corinthians 1:3–5 niv

Give all your worries to Him because He cares for you.
1 Peter 5:7 nlv

"Come to me, all of you who are weary and
carry heavy burdens, and I will give you rest."
Matthew 11:28 nlt

Comfort ye, comfort ye my people, saith your God.
Isaiah 40:1 kjv

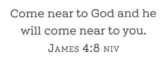

Come near to God and he
will come near to you.
JAMES 4:8 NIV

For the Lord himself will come down from heaven with
a commanding shout, with the voice of the archangel,
and with the trumpet call of God. First, the believers who
have died will rise from their graves. Then, together with
them, we who are still alive and remain on the earth
will be caught up in the clouds to meet the Lord in
the air. Then we will be with the Lord forever.
So encourage each other with these words.
1 THESSALONIANS 4:16–18 NLT

I have remembered Your Law from a long
time ago, O Lord, and I am comforted.
PSALM 119:52 NLV

I will not leave you comfortless: I will come to you.
JOHN 14:18 KJV

When anxiety was great within me,
your consolation brought me joy.
PSALM 94:19 NIV

The Lord GOD will wipe away
tears from off all faces.
ISAIAH 25:8 KJV

You will restore me to even greater
honor and comfort me once again.
PSALM 71:21 NLT

Yea, though I walk through the valley of the shadow
of death, I will fear no evil: for thou art with me;
thy rod and thy staff they comfort me.

PSALM 23:4 KJV

*Dear God, thank You for sending Your Comforter
to soothe my hurting. I don't need to look to earthly friends
for help, although You have given those who support me in
the worst of times. You are always just a prayer away,
and even when I can't think of the right words, You
still understand me. Thank You, Lord. Amen.*

17

Conversation

A fool uttereth all his mind: but a wise
man keepeth it in till afterwards.
PROVERBS 29:11 KJV

A person finds joy in giving an apt reply—
and how good is a timely word!
PROVERBS 15:23 NIV

A gentle answer deflects anger,
but harsh words make tempers flare.
PROVERBS 15:1 NLT

A talebearer revealeth secrets: but he
that is of a faithful spirit concealeth the matter.
PROVERBS 11:13 KJV

There is a time to tear apart, and a time to sew together;
a time to be quiet, and a time to speak.
ECCLESIASTES 3:7 NLV

A word fitly spoken is like apples
of gold in pictures of silver.
PROVERBS 25:11 KJV

Do not be quick with your mouth, do not be hasty in your
heart to utter anything before God. God is in heaven
and you are on earth, so let your words be few.
ECCLESIASTES 5:2 NIV

But now is the time to get rid of anger, rage, malicious
behavior, slander, and dirty language.
COLOSSIANS 3:8 NLT

Even so the tongue is a little member, and boasteth great
things. Behold, how great a matter a little fire kindleth!
JAMES 3:5 KJV

"Whoever would love life and see good days must keep their
tongue from evil and their lips from deceitful speech."
1 Peter 3:10 niv

If I wanted to boast, I would be no fool in doing so, because
I would be telling the truth. But I won't do it, because I don't
want anyone to give me credit beyond what they
can see in my life or hear in my message.
2 Corinthians 12:6 nlt

Anyone who is never at fault in what they say is perfect,
able to keep their whole body in check.
James 3:2 niv

The one who talks much will for sure sin,
but he who is careful what he says is wise.
Proverbs 10:19 nlv

Let your speech be always with grace, seasoned with salt,
that ye may know how ye ought to answer every man.
Colossians 4:6 kjv

Take control of what I say, O Lord, and guard my lips.
PSALM 141:3 NLT

The heart of the righteous weighs its answers,
but the mouth of the wicked gushes evil.
PROVERBS 15:28 NIV

The hearts of the wise make their mouths prudent,
and their lips promote instruction. Gracious words are a
honeycomb, sweet to the soul and healing to the bones.
PROVERBS 16:23–24 NIV

There is one whose foolish words cut like a sword,
but the tongue of the wise brings healing.
PROVERBS 12:18 NLV

*Lord, help me to control my speech. I need Your help in
remembering that even the smallest word can cause great
pain. Guard my tongue, so that I may be a woman of God
who is known as an encourager to others. Amen.*

Counsel

*Whose advice are you taking
and whose example are you watching?*
ANNE GRAHAM LOTZ

Let the wise listen and add to their learning,
and let the discerning get guidance.
PROVERBS 1:5 NIV

And all thy children shall be taught of the LORD;
and great shall be the peace of thy children.
ISAIAH 54:13 KJV

God has given each of you a gift from his great variety of
spiritual gifts. Use them well to serve one another.
1 PETER 4:10 NLT

Brothers and sisters, if someone is caught in a sin,
you who live by the Spirit should restore that person gently.
But watch yourselves, or you also may be tempted.
GALATIANS 6:1 NIV

For unto us a child is born, unto us a son is given: and the
government shall be upon his shoulder: and his name
shall be called Wonderful, Counsellor, The mighty God,
The everlasting Father, The Prince of Peace.

ISAIAH 9:6 KJV

"The Lord disciplines the one he loves, and he chastens
everyone he accepts as his son." Endure hardship
as discipline; God is treating you as his children.
For what children are not disciplined by their father?

HEBREWS 12:6–7 NIV

Instruct the wise, and they will be even wiser.
Teach the righteous, and they will learn even more.

PROVERBS 9:9 NLT

Hear counsel, and receive instruction,
that thou mayest be wise in thy latter end.

PROVERBS 19:20 KJV

"The Holy Spirit is coming. He will lead you into all truth.
He will not speak His Own words. He will speak what
He hears. He will tell you of things to come."

JOHN 16:13 NLV

Now no chastening for the present seemeth to be joyous,
but grievous: nevertheless afterward it yieldeth
the peaceable fruit of righteousness unto
them which are exercised thereby.

HEBREWS 12:11 KJV

Perfume and incense bring joy to the heart, and the
pleasantness of a friend springs from their heartfelt advice.

PROVERBS 27:9 NIV

Fools think their own way is right,
but the wise listen to others.

PROVERBS 12:15 NLT

Where no counsel is, the people fall:
but in the multitude of counsellors there is safety.

PROVERBS 11:14 KJV

Plans go wrong for lack of advice;
many advisers bring success.

PROVERBS 15:22 NLT

*Dear God, I pray that I won't be too proud to ask for help
and advice from others. Please let me be receptive to their
words. When others come to me for counsel, give me
ears to listen and the right words to respond. Amen.*

Courage

Courage is fear that has said its prayers.
ANNE LAMOTT

And now, little children, abide in him; that, when he
shall appear, we may have confidence, and not
be ashamed before him at his coming.
1 JOHN 2:28 KJV

Be strong. Be strong in heart, all you who hope in the Lord.
PSALM 31:24 NLV

For God has not given us a spirit of fear and timidity,
but of power, love, and self-discipline.
2 TIMOTHY 1:7 NLT

Therefore, brothers and sisters, since we have confidence
to enter the Most Holy Place by the blood of Jesus. . .
let us draw near to God with a sincere heart and
with the full assurance that faith brings.
HEBREWS 10:19, 22 NIV

Those who fear the LORD are secure;
he will be a refuge for their children.
PROVERBS 14:26 NLT

In [Jesus] and through faith in him we may approach
God with freedom and confidence.
EPHESIANS 3:12 NIV

Only be thou strong and very courageous, that thou
mayest observe to do according to all the law, which Moses
my servant commanded thee: turn not from it to the
right hand or to the left, that thou mayest
prosper whithersoever thou goest.
JOSHUA 1:7 KJV

So we say with confidence, "The Lord is my helper;
I will not be afraid. What can mere mortals do to me?"
HEBREWS 13:6 NIV

The wicked run away when no one is chasing them,
but the godly are as bold as lions.

Proverbs 28:1 NLT

Wait for the Lord. Be strong. Let your heart
be strong. Yes, wait for the Lord.

Psalm 27:14 NLV

Be on your guard; stand firm in the faith;
be courageous; be strong.

1 Corinthians 16:13 NIV

Father, forgive me when I'm fearful. I know that You are bigger than anything I may encounter in life. Remind me that You have laid out my future, and You already know what is going to happen. I confess my apprehensions. Amen.

Diligence

When I stand before God at the end of my life, I would hope that I would not have a single bit of talent left and could say, "I used everything you gave me."
ERMA BOMBECK

And beside this, giving all diligence, add to your faith virtue;
and to virtue knowledge; and to knowledge temperance;
and to temperance patience; and to patience godliness;
and to godliness brotherly kindness; and to brotherly
kindness charity.... Wherefore the rather, brethren,
give diligence to make your calling and election
sure: for if ye do these things, ye shall never fall.
2 PETER 1:5–7, 10 KJV

Do not let yourselves get tired of doing good.
If we do not give up, we will get what is
coming to us at the right time.
GALATIANS 6:9 NLV

"Be very careful to obey all the commands and the
instructions that Moses gave to you. Love the LORD your God,
walk in all his ways, obey his commands, hold firmly to him,
and serve him with all your heart and all your soul."

JOSHUA 22:5 NLT

This is what I have observed to be good: that it is
appropriate for a person to eat, to drink and to find
satisfaction in their toilsome labor under the sun during
the few days of life God has given them—for this is their lot.
Moreover, when God gives someone wealth and possessions,
and the ability to enjoy them, to accept their lot and
be happy in their toil—this is a gift of God.
ECCLESIASTES 5:18–19 NIV

And as for you, brothers and sisters,
never tire of doing what is good.
2 THESSALONIANS 3:13 NIV

Lazy hands make for poverty,
but diligent hands bring wealth.
PROVERBS 10:4 NIV

I call to remembrance my song in the night: I commune with
mine own heart: and my spirit made diligent search.
PSALM 77:6 KJV

"We must quickly carry out the tasks assigned us by the one
who sent us. The night is coming, and then no one can work."
JOHN 9:4 NLT

Keep thy heart with all diligence;
for out of it are the issues of life.
PROVERBS 4:23 KJV

"Do not work for food that does not last. Work for food that lasts forever. The Son of Man will give you that kind of food. God the Father has shown He will do this."
JOHN 6:27 NLV

If your gift is prophesying, then prophesy in accordance with your faith; if it is serving, then serve; if it is teaching, then teach; if it is to encourage, then give encouragement; if it is giving, then give generously; if it is to lead, do it diligently; if it is to show mercy, do it cheerfully.
ROMANS 12:6–8 NIV

The soul of the sluggard desireth, and hath nothing: but the soul of the diligent shall be made fat.
PROVERBS 13:4 KJV

Good planning and hard work lead to prosperity, but hasty shortcuts lead to poverty.
PROVERBS 21:5 NLT

Therefore, as ye abound in every thing, in faith, and utterance, and knowledge, and in all diligence, and in your love to us, see that ye abound in this grace also.
2 CORINTHIANS 8:7 KJV

Therefore, my dear brothers and sisters, stand firm.
Let nothing move you. Always give yourselves fully
to the work of the Lord, because you know that
your labor in the Lord is not in vain.
1 CORINTHIANS 15:58 NIV

Whatsoever is commanded by the God of heaven,
let it be diligently done for the house of the God of
heaven: for why should there be wrath against
the realm of the king and his sons?
EZRA 7:23 KJV

Dear friends, since you are waiting for these things to
happen, do all you can to be found by Him in peace.
2 PETER 3:14 NLV

*Thank You for opportunities, Jesus. Day by day
through study and work, help me to reach
higher levels of character. In my climb,
Lord, guide me to great heights. Amen.*

Discipline, God's

*God has to punish His children from time to time
and it is the very demonstration of His love.*
ELISABETH ELLIOT

As many as I love, I rebuke and chasten:
be zealous therefore, and repent.
REVELATION 3:19 KJV

"Blessed is the one whom God corrects; so do not despise
the discipline of the Almighty. For he wounds, but he
also binds up; he injures, but his hands also heal."
JOB 5:17–18 NIV

Joyful are those you discipline, LORD, those you teach with
your instructions. You give them relief from troubled
times until a pit is dug to capture the wicked.
PSALM 94:12–13 NLT

But if we would look into our own lives and see if we
are guilty, then God would not have to say we are guilty.
When we are guilty, we are punished by the Lord so we
will not be told we are guilty with the rest of the world.

1 Corinthians 11:31–32 nlv

For the commandment is a lamp; and the law is light;
and reproofs of instruction are the way of life.

Proverbs 6:23 kjv

The Lord disciplines those he loves,
as a father the son he delights in.

Proverbs 3:12 niv

No discipline is enjoyable while it is happening—it's painful!
But afterward there will be a peaceful harvest of right
living for those who are trained in this way.

Hebrews 12:11 nlt

O Lord, do not speak sharp words to me in Your anger,
or punish me when You are angry.
PSALM 6:1 NLV

The LORD hath chastened me sore:
but he hath not given me over unto death.
PSALM 118:18 KJV

"Think about it: Just as a parent disciplines a child,
the LORD your God disciplines you for your own good."
DEUTERONOMY 8:5 NLT

*Thank You, God, for Your correction when I make the
wrong choices. Discipline hurts, but I pray that it will
teach me to stay close to You and not wander out
on my own. May I learn to obey You. Amen.*

Encouragement

Give a little of yourself, even though you feel stretched already. One certain way to receive encouragement, hope, or companionship is to give it.
GRETCHEN THOMPSON

Carry each other's burdens,
and in this way you will fulfill the law of Christ.
GALATIANS 6:2 NIV

Even when we are weighed down with troubles, it is for your comfort and salvation! For when we ourselves are comforted, we will certainly comfort you. Then you can patiently endure the same things we suffer.
2 CORINTHIANS 1:6 NLT

All scripture is given by inspiration of God,
and is profitable for doctrine, for reproof,
for correction, for instruction in righteousness.
2 TIMOTHY 3:16 KJV

Not giving up meeting together, as some are in the habit of doing, but encouraging one another—and all the more as you see the Day approaching.
HEBREWS 10:25 NIV

"When they take you to the places of worship and to the courts and to the leaders of the country, do not be worried about what you should say or how to say it. The Holy Spirit will tell you what you should say at that time."
LUKE 12:11–12 NLV

Brethren, if any of you do err from the truth, and one convert him; let him know, that he which converteth the sinner from the error of his way shall save a soul from death, and shall hide a multitude of sins.
JAMES 5:19–20 KJV

But encourage one another daily, as long as it is called "Today," so that none of you may be hardened by sin's deceitfulness.
HEBREWS 3:13 NIV

In each city they helped the Christians to be strong and true to the faith. They told them, "We must suffer many hard things to get into the holy nation of God."
ACTS 14:22 NLV

He must have a strong belief in the trustworthy message he was taught; then he will be able to encourage others with wholesome teaching and show those who oppose it where they are wrong.
TITUS 1:9 NLT

I can do all things through Christ which strengtheneth me.
PHILIPPIANS 4:13 KJV

With all these things in mind, dear brothers and sisters,
stand firm and keep a strong grip on the teaching we passed
on to you both in person and by letter. Now may our Lord
Jesus Christ himself and God our Father, who loved us
and by his grace gave us eternal comfort and a
wonderful hope, comfort you and strengthen
you in every good thing you do and say.
2 THESSALONIANS 2:15–17 NLT

Wherefore comfort yourselves together,
and edify one another, even as also ye do.
1 THESSALONIANS 5:11 KJV

*Lord Jesus, thank You for the encouraging words
that others have for me. I pray that I will be
an encouragement to others as well. Amen.*

Eternity

*With Christ as your Companion,
you are a creature of eternity.*

EDITH MARGARET CLARKSON

And this world is fading away, along with everything
that people crave. But anyone who does
what pleases God will live forever.

1 JOHN 2:17 NLT

And I give unto them eternal life; and they shall never
perish, neither shall any man pluck them out of my hand.

JOHN 10:28 KJV

Then I saw a new heaven and a new earth. The first heaven
and the first earth had passed away. There was no more sea.
I saw the Holy City, the new Jerusalem. It was coming
down out of heaven from God. It was made ready
like a bride is made ready for her husband.

REVELATION 21:1–2 NLV

And there shall be no night there; and they need no candle, neither light of the sun; for the Lord God giveth them light: and they shall reign for ever and ever.

REVELATION 22:5 KJV

"Multitudes who sleep in the dust of the earth will awake: some to everlasting life, others to shame and everlasting contempt."

DANIEL 12:2 NIV

And when the Great Shepherd appears, you will receive a crown of never-ending glory and honor.

1 PETER 5:4 NLT

Listen, I tell you a mystery: We will not all sleep, but we will all be changed—in a flash, in the twinkling of an eye, at the last trumpet. For the trumpet will sound, the dead will be raised imperishable, and we will be changed. For the perishable must clothe itself with the imperishable, and the mortal with immortality. When the perishable has been clothed with the imperishable, and the mortal with immortality, then the saying that is written will come true: "Death has been swallowed up in victory."

1 CORINTHIANS 15:51–54 NIV

Blessed be the God and Father of our Lord Jesus Christ, which according to his abundant mercy hath begotten us again unto a lively hope by the resurrection of Jesus Christ from the dead, to an inheritance incorruptible, and undefiled, and that fadeth not away, reserved in heaven for you, who are kept by the power of God through faith unto salvation ready to be revealed in the last time.

1 PETER 1:3–5 KJV

The Holy Spirit raised Jesus from the dead.
If the same Holy Spirit lives in you, He will
give life to your bodies in the same way.

ROMANS 8:11 NLV

For the wages of sin is death, but the gift
of God is eternal life in Christ Jesus our Lord.

ROMANS 6:23 NIV

For we know that when this earthly tent we live in is taken
down (that is, when we die and leave this earthly body),
we will have a house in heaven, an eternal body made
for us by God himself and not by human hands.

2 CORINTHIANS 5:1 NLT

God. . .will render to every man according to his deeds: to them who by patient continuance in well doing seek for glory and honour and immortality, eternal life.

ROMANS 2:5–7 KJV

"Anyone who loves their life will lose it, while anyone who hates their life in this world will keep it for eternal life."

JOHN 12:25 NIV

Those who live to please the Spirit will harvest everlasting life from the Spirit.

GALATIANS 6:8 NLT

There is a crown which comes from being right with God. The Lord, the One Who will judge, will give it to me on that great day when He comes again. I will not be the only one to receive a crown. All those who love to think of His coming and are looking for Him will receive one also.

2 TIMOTHY 4:8 NLV

"My Father's house has many rooms; if that were not so, would I have told you that I am going there to prepare a place for you? And if I go and prepare a place for you, I will come back and take you to be with me that you also may be where I am."

JOHN 14:2–3 NIV

Jesus said unto her, I am the resurrection, and the life: he that believeth in me, though he were dead, yet shall he live: And whosoever liveth and believeth in me shall never die. Believest thou this?

JOHN 11:25–26 KJV

"Do not work for food that does not last. Work for food that lasts forever. The Son of Man will give you that kind of food. God the Father has shown He will do this."

JOHN 6:27 NLV

We are looking forward to the new heavens and new earth he has promised, a world filled with God's righteousness.

2 PETER 3:13 NLT

Search the scriptures; for in them ye think ye have
eternal life: and they are they which testify of me.

JOHN 5:39 KJV

"They are before the throne of God and serve him day
and night in his temple; and he who sits on the throne
will shelter them with his presence. 'Never again will they
hunger; never again will they thirst. The sun will not beat
down on them,' nor any scorching heat. For the Lamb at
the center of the throne will be their shepherd; 'he will
lead them to springs of living water.' 'And God
will wipe away every tear from their eyes.' "

REVELATION 7:15–17 NIV

"For sure, I tell you, anyone who hears My Word and puts his
trust in Him Who sent Me has life that lasts forever. He will
not be guilty. He has already passed from death into life."

JOHN 5:24 NLV

*Lord God, I feel so special when I think that You are
preparing a place in heaven for me. To be considered Your
child is overwhelming, as You have chosen me to be a part
of Your family. I long to be in Your presence, laying my
crown at Your feet, and worshipping You forever. Amen.*

Faith

God loves it when you and I step into the pitch-black night of this world with the candle of His presence.
ANGELA THOMAS

The Lord answered, "If you had faith even as small as a mustard seed, you could say to this mulberry tree, 'May you be uprooted and be planted in the sea,' and it would obey you!"
LUKE 17:6 NLT

Ask in faith, nothing wavering. For he that wavereth is like a wave of the sea driven with the wind and tossed.
JAMES 1:6 KJV

You have never seen Him but you love Him. You cannot see Him now but you are putting your trust in Him. And you have joy so great that words cannot tell about it.
1 PETER 1:8 NLV

Jesus told him, "Don't be afraid; just believe."
MARK 5:36 NIV

And he said to the woman,
Thy faith hath saved thee; go in peace.
LUKE 7:50 KJV

For you are all children of God through faith in Christ Jesus.
GALATIANS 3:26 NLT

But as many as received him, to them gave he power
to become the sons of God, even to them
that believe on his name.
JOHN 1:12 KJV

"Whoever believes and is baptized will be saved,
but whoever does not believe will be condemned."
MARK 16:16 NIV

Now faith is being sure we will get what we hope for.
It is being sure of what we cannot see.
HEBREWS 11:1 NLV

Then Christ will make his home in your hearts as you trust
in him. Your roots will grow down into God's love and keep
you strong. And may you have the power to understand,
as all God's people should, how wide, how long, how high,
and how deep his love is. May you experience the love
of Christ, though it is too great to understand fully.
Then you will be made complete with all the fullness
of life and power that comes from God.
EPHESIANS 3:17–19 NLT

" 'If you can'?" said Jesus.
"Everything is possible for one who believes."
MARK 9:23 NIV

It is written in the prophets, And they shall be all
taught of God. Every man therefore that hath heard,
and hath learned of the Father, cometh unto me.
JOHN 6:45 KJV

In this way, you do not have faith in Christ
because of the wisdom of men. You have faith
in Christ because of the power of God.
1 CORINTHIANS 2:5 NLV

Be on your guard; stand firm in the faith;
be courageous; be strong.

1 CORINTHIANS 16:13 NIV

That if thou shalt confess with thy mouth the Lord Jesus,
and shalt believe in thine heart that God hath raised
him from the dead, thou shalt be saved.

ROMANS 10:9 KJV

Then Jesus said to the disciples, "Have faith in God. I tell you
the truth, you can say to this mountain, 'May you be lifted up
and thrown into the sea,' and it will happen. But you must
really believe it will happen and have no doubt in your heart."

MARK 11:22–23 NLT

For by His loving-favor you have been saved from
the punishment of sin through faith. It is not by
anything you have done. It is a gift of God.

EPHESIANS 2:8 NLV

Then Jesus told him, "Because you have seen me,
you have believed; blessed are those who
have not seen and yet have believed."

JOHN 20:29 NIV

But without faith it is impossible to please him: for he that
cometh to God must believe that he is, and that he is
a rewarder of them that diligently seek him.

HEBREWS 11:6 KJV

Jesus answered, "The work of God is this:
to believe in the one he has sent."

JOHN 6:29 NIV

Let us go right into the presence of God with sincere hearts
fully trusting him. For our guilty consciences have been
sprinkled with Christ's blood to make us clean, and our
bodies have been washed with pure water.

HEBREWS 10:22 NLT

Whoever believes in the Son of God accepts this testimony.
Whoever does not believe God has made him out to
be a liar, because they have not believed the
testimony God has given about his Son.

1 JOHN 5:10 NIV

As you have put your trust in Christ Jesus the Lord
to save you from the punishment of sin,
now let Him lead you in every step.

COLOSSIANS 2:6 NLV

"Here I am! I stand at the door and knock. If anyone hears
my voice and opens the door, I will come in and
eat with that person, and they with me."
REVELATION 3:20 NIV

Jesus saith unto her, Said I not unto thee, that, if thou
wouldest believe, thou shouldest see the glory of God?
JOHN 11:40 KJV

My old self has been crucified with Christ. It is no longer
I who live, but Christ lives in me. So I live in this earthly
body by trusting in the Son of God, who loved
me and gave himself for me.
GALATIANS 2:20 NLT

For we walk by faith, not by sight.
2 CORINTHIANS 5:7 KJV

*Father, please help me to be a woman of faith, believing that
You will work all details out in my life. Let me not rely on
tangible, explainable things, but to remember that You are
in control of everything–known and unknown. Amen.*

Faithfulness of God

When your friends and loved ones fail you,
God remains by your side, steadfast and true.
LIZ CURTIS HIGGS

For the LORD your God is a merciful God; he will not
abandon or destroy you or forget the covenant with
your ancestors, which he confirmed to them by oath.
DEUTERONOMY 4:31 NIV

And the heavens shall praise thy wonders, O LORD:
thy faithfulness also in the congregation of the saints.
PSALM 89:5 KJV

And we know that God causes everything to work
together for the good of those who love God and
are called according to his purpose for them.
ROMANS 8:28 NLT

"Be faithful even to death.
Then I will give you the crown of life."
REVELATION 2:10 NLV

"Praise be to the LORD, who has given rest to his people Israel just as he promised. Not one word has failed of all the good promises he gave through his servant Moses."

1 KINGS 8:56 NIV

God is not a man, that he should lie; neither the son of man, that he should repent: hath he said, and shall he not do it? or hath he spoken, and shall he not make it good?

NUMBERS 23:19 KJV

If we have no faith, He will still be faithful for He cannot go against what He is.

2 TIMOTHY 2:13 NLV

This truth gives them confidence that they have eternal life, which God—who does not lie—promised them before the world began.

TITUS 1:2 NLT

Know therefore that the LORD thy God, he is God, the faithful God, which keepeth covenant and mercy with them that love him and keep his commandments to a thousand generations.

DEUTERONOMY 7:9 KJV

Let us hold unswervingly to the hope we profess,
for he who promised is faithful.

HEBREWS 10:23 NIV

Love the Lord, all you who belong to Him! The Lord keeps
the faithful safe. But He gives the proud their pay in full.

PSALM 31:23 NLV

The Lord isn't really being slow about his promise,
as some people think. No, he is being patient
for your sake. He does not want anyone to be
destroyed, but wants everyone to repent.

2 PETER 3:9 NLT

So this is what the Sovereign LORD says: "See, I lay a stone
in Zion, a tested stone, a precious cornerstone for
a sure foundation; the one who relies on it
will never be stricken with panic."

ISAIAH 28:16 NIV

Thank You, Lord, for remaining steadfast. Nothing else in my life is as sure as You. I am grateful that You will never leave me, regardless of what I do. I love You, Lord! Amen.

Forgiveness

As we practice the work of forgiveness, we discover
more and more that forgiveness and healing are one.
Agnes Sanford

And be ye kind one to another, tenderhearted, forgiving one
another, even as God for Christ's sake hath forgiven you.
Ephesians 4:32 kjv

"Forgive us our sins as we forgive those who sin against us."
Matthew 6:12 nlv

"Forgive us our sins, as we forgive those who sin against us.
And don't let us yield to temptation."

Luke 11:4 nlt

Then [Jesus] turned toward the woman and said to Simon, "Do you see this woman? I came into your house. You did not give me any water for my feet, but she wet my feet with her tears and wiped them with her hair. You did not give me a kiss, but this woman, from the time I entered, has not stopped kissing my feet. You did not put oil on my head, but she has poured perfume on my feet. Therefore, I tell you, her many sins have been forgiven—as her great love has shown. But whoever has been forgiven little loves little." Then Jesus said to her, "Your sins are forgiven."

LUKE 7:44–48 NIV

And when ye stand praying, forgive, if ye have ought against any: that your Father also which is in heaven may forgive you your trespasses. But if ye do not forgive, neither will your Father which is in heaven forgive your trespasses.

MARK 11:25–26 KJV

"But I say, do not resist an evil person! If someone slaps you on the right cheek, offer the other cheek also. If you are sued in court and your shirt is taken from you, give your coat, too. If a soldier demands that you carry his gear for a mile, carry it two miles."

MATTHEW 5:39–41 NLT

"For if you forgive other people when they sin against you, your heavenly Father will also forgive you. But if you do not forgive others their sins, your Father will not forgive your sins."
MATTHEW 6:14–15 NIV

For thou, Lord, art good, and ready to forgive; and plenteous in mercy unto all them that call upon thee.
PSALM 86:5 KJV

Try to understand other people. Forgive each other. If you have something against someone, forgive him. That is the way the Lord forgave you.
COLOSSIANS 3:13 NLV

"Then if my people who are called by my name will humble themselves and pray and seek my face and turn from their wicked ways, I will hear from heaven and will forgive their sins and restore their land."
2 CHRONICLES 7:14 NLT

Judge not, and ye shall not be judged: condemn not, and ye shall not be condemned: forgive, and ye shall be forgiven.
LUKE 6:37 KJV

When someone does something bad to you, do not do the same thing to him. When someone talks about you, do not talk about him. Instead, pray that good will come to him. You were called to do this so you might receive good things from God.

1 PETER 3:9 NLV

"If your brother or sister sins against you, rebuke them; and if they repent, forgive them. Even if they sin against you seven times in a day and seven times come back to you saying 'I repent,' you must forgive them."

LUKE 17:3–4 NIV

Sensible people control their temper;
they earn respect by overlooking wrongs.

PROVERBS 19:11 NLT

Then came Peter to him, and said, Lord, how oft shall my brother sin against me, and I forgive him? till seven times? Jesus saith unto him, I say not unto thee, Until seven times: but, Until seventy times seven.

MATTHEW 18:21–22 KJV

Dear God, forgive me for sinning against You. It hurts me to know that I've failed You, the One who has given me the gift of new life. When others wound me, may I extend to them the same forgiveness that You grant to me. Amen.

Friendship

*Life is partly what we make it, and partly
it is made by the friends we choose.*
TRACI MULLINS

Don't you realize that friendship with the world makes you
an enemy of God? I say it again: If you want to be a friend
of the world, you make yourself an enemy of God.
JAMES 4:4 NLT

As iron sharpens iron, so one person sharpens another.
PROVERBS 27:17 NIV

A friend loveth at all times.
PROVERBS 17:17 KJV

There are "friends" who destroy each other,
but a real friend sticks closer than a brother.
PROVERBS 18:24 NLT

"Kindness from a friend should be shown to a man
without hope, or he might turn away from
the fear of the All-powerful."
JOB 6:14 NLV

Faithful are the wounds of a friend.
PROVERBS 27:6 KJV

*Heavenly Father, I praise You for the friends
You've provided for me. Bless them for
their investment in my life. Amen.*

Generosity

Beyond giving of our material possessions,
God calls upon us to give ourselves
away—our time, energy, and passion.
Jill Briscoe

Then a poor widow came by and dropped in two small
coins. "I tell you the truth," Jesus said, "this poor widow
has given more than all the rest of them. For they have
given a tiny part of their surplus, but she, poor as
she is, has given everything she has."
Luke 21:2–4 nlt

"If any of your fellow Israelites become poor and are
unable to support themselves among you, help them
as you would a foreigner and stranger, so they
can continue to live among you."
Leviticus 25:35 niv

Blessed are those who have regard for the weak; the Lord delivers them in times of trouble. The Lord protects and preserves them—they are counted among the blessed in the land—he does not give them over to the desire of their foes.

PSALM 41:1–2 NIV

But when thou makest a feast, call the poor, the maimed, the lame, the blind: And thou shalt be blessed; for they cannot recompense thee: for thou shalt be recompensed at the resurrection of the just.

LUKE 14:13–14 KJV

Tell those who are rich in this world not to be proud and not to trust in their money. Money cannot be trusted. They should put their trust in God. He gives us all we need for our happiness. Tell them to do good and be rich in good works. They should give much to those in need and be ready to share.

1 TIMOTHY 6:17–18 NLV

Each of you should give what you have decided
in your heart to give, not reluctantly or under
compulsion, for God loves a cheerful giver.

2 CORINTHIANS 9:7 NIV

All must give as they are able, according to the blessings
given to them by the LORD your God.

DEUTERONOMY 16:17 NLT

For the poor shall never cease out of the land: therefore I
command thee, saying, Thou shalt open thine hand wide
unto thy brother, to thy poor, and to thy needy, in thy land.

DEUTERONOMY 15:11 KJV

"Truly I tell you, anyone who gives you a cup of water in
my name because you belong to the Messiah
will certainly not lose their reward."

MARK 9:41 NIV

You know of the loving-favor shown by our Lord Jesus Christ.
He was rich, but He became poor for your good. In that way,
because He became poor, you might become rich.

2 CORINTHIANS 8:9 NLV

"Give, and you will receive. Your gift will return to you in full—pressed down, shaken together to make room for more, running over, and poured into your lap. The amount you give will determine the amount you get back."

LUKE 6:38 NLT

John answered, "Anyone who has two shirts should share with the one who has none, and anyone who has food should do the same."

LUKE 3:11 NIV

They have freely scattered their gifts to the poor, their righteousness endures forever; their horn will be lifted high in honor.

PSALM 112:9 NIV

It is a sin to belittle one's neighbor; blessed are those who help the poor.

PROVERBS 14:21 NLT

I have shewed you all things, how that so labouring ye
ought to support the weak, and to remember the
words of the Lord Jesus, how he said, It is
more blessed to give than to receive.
Acts 20:35 kjv

If a brother or sister be naked, and destitute of daily food,
and one of you say unto them, Depart in peace, be ye
warmed and filled; notwithstanding ye give them not those
things which are needful to the body; what doth it profit?
James 2:15–16 kjv

If you have any women whose husbands have died in
your family, you must care for them. The church should
not have to help them. The church can help women
whose husbands have died who are all alone in
this world and have no one else to help them.
1 Timothy 5:16 nlv

"Share your food with the hungry, and give shelter to the homeless. Give clothes to those who need them, and do not hide from relatives who need your help. Then your salvation will come like the dawn, and your wounds will quickly heal. Your godliness will lead you forward, and the glory of the LORD will protect you from behind."

ISAIAH 58:7–8 NLT

Therefore when thou doest thine alms, do not sound a trumpet before thee, as the hypocrites do in the synagogues and in the streets, that they may have glory of men. Verily I say unto you, They have their reward. But when thou doest alms, let not thy left hand know what thy right hand doeth: That thine alms may be in secret: and thy Father which seeth in secret himself shall reward thee openly.

MATTHEW 6:2–4 KJV

Do not withhold good from those to whom it is due, when it is in your power to act. Do not say to your neighbor, "Come back tomorrow and I'll give it to you"—when you already have it with you.

PROVERBS 3:27–28 NIV

Father, I want to share all of the blessings You've given to me with others. Loosen my grip when I grasp them too tightly. I will experience joy when I share what I have with others. Amen.

Gentleness

Take my heart and make it Your dwelling place so that everyone I touch will be touched also by You!
ALICE JOYCE DAVIDSON

And the Lord's servant must not be quarrelsome but must be kind to everyone, able to teach, not resentful. Opponents must be gently instructed, in the hope that God will grant them repentance leading them to a knowledge of the truth, and that they will come to their senses and escape from the trap of the devil, who has taken them captive to do his will.
2 TIMOTHY 2:24–26 NIV

But the fruit of the Spirit is love, joy, peace, longsuffering, gentleness, goodness, faith.
GALATIANS 5:22 KJV

The lowly will possess the land and will live in peace and prosperity.
PSALM 37:11 NLT

But the wisdom that comes from heaven is first of all pure.
Then it gives peace. It is gentle and willing to obey. It is full
of loving-kindness and of doing good. It has no doubts
and does not pretend to be something it is not.

JAMES 3:17 NLV

But we were gentle among you, even as a nurse cherisheth
her children: So being affectionately desirous of you,
we were willing to have imparted unto you, not the
gospel of God only, but also our own souls.

1 THESSALONIANS 2:7–8 KJV

For the LORD taketh pleasure in his people:
he will beautify the meek with salvation.

PSALM 149:4 KJV

He tends his flock like a shepherd: He gathers the
lambs in his arms and carries them close to his
heart; he gently leads those that have young.

ISAIAH 40:11 NIV

Now I, Paul, appeal to you with the gentleness and
kindness of Christ—though I realize you think I am timid
in person and bold only when I write from far away.

2 CORINTHIANS 10:1 NLT

Teach your people to obey the leaders of their country. They should be ready to do any good work. They must not speak bad of anyone, and they must not argue. They should be gentle and kind to all people.

TITUS 3:1–2 NLV

Take my yoke upon you, and learn of me; for I am meek and lowly in heart: and ye shall find rest unto your souls.

MATTHEW 11:29 KJV

The LORD supports the humble, but he brings the wicked down into the dust.

PSALM 147:6 NLT

The meek will he guide in judgment: and the meek will he teach his way.

PSALM 25:9 KJV

Sometimes when life gets overwhelming, I lose patience, Father. Help me to react with a gentle spirit. When I choose gentleness, my circumstances and attitude improve. Ripen the fruit of gentleness in my life. Amen.

God's Love

*God's love, pouring through the lonely life of Jesus,
runs deeper, wider, and farther than any
loneliness of the human heart.*

BONNIE KEEN

And hope maketh not ashamed; because the love
of God is shed abroad in our hearts by the Holy
Ghost which is given unto us.

ROMANS 5:5 KJV

And so we know and rely on the love God has for us.
God is love. Whoever lives in love lives
in God, and God in them.

1 JOHN 4:16 NIV

See what great love the Father has for us that He
would call us His children. And that is what we are.

1 JOHN 3:1 NLV

But as it is written, Eye hath not seen, nor ear heard, neither have entered into the heart of man, the things which God hath prepared for them that love him.

1 CORINTHIANS 2:9 KJV

But God showed his great love for us by sending Christ to die for us while we were still sinners.

ROMANS 5:8 NLT

For God so loved the world, that he gave his only begotten Son, that whosoever believeth in him should not perish, but have everlasting life.

JOHN 3:16 KJV

For I am convinced that neither death nor life, neither angels nor demons, neither the present nor the future, nor any powers, neither height nor depth, nor anything else in all creation, will be able to separate us from the love of God that is in Christ Jesus our Lord.

ROMANS 8:38–39 NIV

"The Father loves you. He loves you because you love Me and believe that I came from the Father."

JOHN 16:27 NLV

Herein is love, not that we loved God, but that he loved us,
and sent his Son to be the propitiation for our sins.

1 JOHN 4:10 KJV

The LORD says, "Then I will heal you of your faithlessness; my
love will know no bounds, for my anger will be gone forever."

HOSEA 14:4 NLT

This is how God showed his love among us: He sent his one
and only Son into the world that we might live through him.

1 JOHN 4:9 NIV

The LORD preserveth all them that love him.

PSALM 145:20 KJV

*Lord, at times when I feel unlovable,
thank You for encompassing me with Your love. Amen.*

Gratitude

*We can thank God for everything good,
and all the rest we don't comprehend yet.*
KRISTIN ARMSTRONG

And [Jesus] took the cup, and gave thanks,
and gave it to them, saying, Drink ye all of it.
MATTHEW 26:27 KJV

Then He took the seven loaves of bread and the fish
and gave thanks. He broke them and gave them to His
followers. The followers gave them to the people.
MATTHEW 15:36 NLV

They worshiped together at the Temple each day, met in
homes for the Lord's Supper, and shared their meals with
great joy and generosity—all the while praising God and
enjoying the goodwill of all the people. And each day the
Lord added to their fellowship those who were being saved.

ACTS 2:46–47 NLT

"Praise be to the Lord, who has given rest to his people Israel just as he promised. Not one word has failed of all the good promises he gave through his servant Moses."

1 Kings 8:56 NIV

Blessed be the Lord, who daily loadeth us with benefits, even the God of our salvation. Selah.

Psalm 68:19 KJV

Always give thanks for all things to God the Father in the name of our Lord Jesus Christ.

Ephesians 5:20 NLV

Those who worship the Lord on a special day do it to honor him. Those who eat any kind of food do so to honor the Lord, since they give thanks to God before eating. And those who refuse to eat certain foods also want to please the Lord and give thanks to God.

Romans 14:6 NLT

"I thank and praise you, God of my ancestors: You have given me wisdom and power, you have made known to me what we asked of you, you have made known to us the dream of the king."

Daniel 2:23 NIV

I will mention the lovingkindnesses of the Lord, and the praises of the Lord, according to all that the Lord hath bestowed on us, and the great goodness toward the house of Israel, which he hath bestowed on them according to his mercies, and according to the multitude of his lovingkindnesses.

ISAIAH 63:7 KJV

I will give thanks to the Lord with all my heart. I will tell of all the great things You have done. I will be glad and full of joy because of You. I will sing praise to Your name, O Most High.

PSALM 9:1–2 NLV

Be thankful in all circumstances, for this is God's will for you who belong to Christ Jesus.

1 THESSALONIANS 5:18 NLT

It is good to praise the Lord and make music to your name, O Most High, proclaiming your love in the morning and your faithfulness at night.

PSALM 92:1–2 NIV

Many, O Lord my God, are thy wonderful works which thou
hast done, and thy thoughts which are to us-ward: they
cannot be reckoned up in order unto thee: if I would declare
and speak of them, they are more than can be numbered.

PSALM 40:5 KJV

Give thanks to the Lord, for He is good,
for His loving-kindness lasts forever.

PSALM 136:1 NLV

Singing a song of thanksgiving
and telling of all your wonders.

PSALM 26:7 NLT

You turned my wailing into dancing; you removed
my sackcloth and clothed me with joy, that my
heart may sing your praises and not be silent.
Lord my God, I will praise you forever.

PSALM 30:11–12 NIV

*Forgive me for the times I'm ungrateful, Lord. I don't intend
to take Your love and blessings for granted. Teach me to
express my thanks—to You and to others. Amen.*

Honesty

*Honesty, or dishonesty,
is shown in every little act of life.*
MABEL HALE

Be of the same mind one toward
another.... Recompense to no man evil for evil.
Provide things honest in the sight of all men.
ROMANS 12:16–17 KJV

So I strive always to keep my
conscience clear before God and man.
ACTS 24:16 NIV

Therefore all things whatsoever ye would that men
should do to you, do ye even so to them:
for this is the law and the prophets.
MATTHEW 7:12 KJV

And now, dear brothers and sisters, one final thing.
Fix your thoughts on what is true, and honorable,
and right, and pure, and lovely, and admirable.
Think about things that are excellent
and worthy of praise.

PHILIPPIANS 4:8 NLT

Who may go up the mountain of the Lord? And who may
stand in His holy place? He who has clean hands and a pure
heart. He who has not lifted up his soul to what is
not true, and has not made false promises.

PSALM 24:3–4 NLV

Who lends money to the poor without interest;
who does not accept a bribe against the innocent.
Whoever does these things will never be shaken.

PSALM 15:5 NIV

Those who are honest and fair, who refuse to profit by fraud,
who stay far away from bribes, who refuse to listen to those
who plot murder, who shut their eyes to all enticement to do
wrong—these are the ones who will dwell on high. The rocks
of the mountains will be their fortress. Food will be supplied
to them, and they will have water in abundance.

ISAIAH 33:15–16 NLT

Lie not one to another, seeing that ye have put off the
old man with his deeds; and have put on the new
man, which is renewed in knowledge after
the image of him that created him.
COLOSSIANS 3:9–10 KJV

"I will maintain my innocence and never let go of it;
my conscience will not reproach me as long as I live."
JOB 27:6 NIV

Pray for us. Our hearts tell us we are right.
We want to do the right thing always.
HEBREWS 13:18 NLV

We are careful to be honorable before the Lord,
but we also want everyone else to see
that we are honorable.
2 CORINTHIANS 8:21 NLT

Receive us; we have wronged no man, we have
corrupted no man, we have defrauded no man.

2 CORINTHIANS 7:2 KJV

Slaves, obey your earthly masters in everything; and do it,
not only when their eye is on you and to curry their favor,
but with sincerity of heart and reverence for the Lord.

COLOSSIANS 3:22 NIV

That ye study to be quiet, and to do your own business,
and to work with your own hands. . . . That ye may
walk honestly toward them that are without,
and that ye may have lack of nothing.

1 THESSALONIANS 4:11–12 KJV

The night is almost gone; the day of salvation will soon be
here. So remove your dark deeds like dirty clothes, and put
on the shining armor of right living. Because we belong
to the day, we must live decent lives for all to see.
Don't participate in the darkness of wild parties
and drunkenness, or in sexual promiscuity and
immoral living, or in quarreling and jealousy.

ROMANS 13:12–13 NLT

Tax-gatherers came to be baptized also. They asked [John the Baptist], "Teacher, what are we to do?" He said to them, "Do not take more money from people than you should."

LUKE 3:12–13 NLV

"You know the commandments: 'You shall not murder, you shall not commit adultery, you shall not steal, you shall not give false testimony, you shall not defraud, honor your father and mother.' "

MARK 10:19 NIV

"Do not steal. Do not deceive or cheat one another."

LEVITICUS 19:11 NLT

Heavenly Father, it seems that it's becoming increasingly acceptable to speak "partial truths," especially to avoid offending others. But anything less than complete honesty offends You. Help me to be a woman of honesty. Amen.

Hope

*There is no safer place for your hopes and dreams
than in the loving hands of your faithful Father.*
LESLIE LUDY

According to my earnest expectation and my hope, that in
nothing I shall be ashamed, but that with all boldness,
as always, so now also Christ shall be magnified in my
body, whether it be by life, or by death.
PHILIPPIANS 1:20 KJV

Not only so, but we also glory in our sufferings, because we
know that suffering produces perseverance; perseverance,
character; and character, hope. And hope does not put us
to shame, because God's love has been poured out into our
hearts through the Holy Spirit, who has been given to us.
ROMANS 5:3–5 NIV

And we desire that every one of you do shew the same
diligence to the full assurance of hope unto the end.
HEBREWS 6:11 KJV

"I have the same hope in God that these men have,
that he will raise both the righteous and the unrighteous."
ACTS 24:15 NLT

Dear friends, now we are children of God, and what we
will be has not yet been made known. But we know that
when Christ appears, we shall be like him, for we shall
see him as he is. All who have this hope in him
purify themselves, just as he is pure.
1 JOHN 3:2–3 NIV

Let us thank the God and Father of our Lord Jesus Christ.
It was through His loving-kindness that we were born again
to a new life and have a hope that never dies. This hope
is ours because Jesus was raised from the dead.
1 PETER 1:3 NLV

Blessed is the man that trusteth
in the LORD, and whose hope the LORD is.
JEREMIAH 17:7 KJV

But Christ, as the Son, is in charge of God's entire house.
And we are God's house, if we keep our courage
and remain confident in our hope in Christ.
HEBREWS 3:6 NLT

But I will hope continually,
and will yet praise thee more and more.
PSALM 71:14 KJV

Brothers and sisters, we do not want you to be uninformed
about those who sleep in death, so that you do not grieve
like the rest of mankind, who have no hope. For we believe
that Jesus died and rose again, and so we believe that God
will bring with Jesus those who have fallen asleep in him.
1 THESSALONIANS 4:13–14 NIV

But since we belong to the day, let us be sober
putting on faith and love as a breastplate,
and the hope of salvation as a helmet.
1 THESSALONIANS 5:8 NIV

But sanctify the Lord God in your hearts: and be ready always to give an answer to every man that asketh you a reason of the hope that is in you with meekness and fear.

1 PETER 3:15 KJV

We thank God for the hope that is being kept for you in heaven. You first heard about this hope through the Good News which is the Word of Truth.

COLOSSIANS 1:5 NLV

For we are saved by hope: but hope that is seen is not hope: for what a man seeth, why doth he yet hope for? But if we hope for that we see not, then do we with patience wait for it.

ROMANS 8:24–25 KJV

We are waiting for the hope of being made right with God. This will come through the Holy Spirit and by faith.

GALATIANS 5:5 NLV

In hope of eternal life, which God, that cannot lie,
promised before the world began.

TITUS 1:2 KJV

We wait for the blessed hope—the appearing of the
glory of our great God and Savior, Jesus Christ.

TITUS 2:13 NIV

LORD, I have hoped for thy salvation,
and done thy commandments.

PSALM 119:166 KJV

My soul becomes weak with desire for Your saving power,
but I have put my hope in Your Word.

PSALM 119:81 NLV

Now faith is confidence in what we hope for
and assurance about what we do not see.

HEBREWS 11:1 NIV

I pray that God, the source of hope, will fill you completely
with joy and peace because you trust in him. Then you
will overflow with confident hope through
the power of the Holy Spirit.

ROMANS 15:13 NLT

Remember your word to your servant,
for you have given me hope.

PSALM 119:49 NIV

Seeing then that we have such hope,
we use great plainness of speech.

2 CORINTHIANS 3:12 KJV

God gave these two things that cannot be changed and
God cannot lie. We who have turned to Him can have great
comfort knowing that He will do what He has promised.
This hope is a safe anchor for our souls. It will never
move. This hope goes into the Holiest Place
of All behind the curtain of heaven.

HEBREWS 6:18–19 NLV

I pray that your hearts will be flooded with light so that
you can understand the confident hope he has given
to those he called—his holy people who are
his rich and glorious inheritance.

EPHESIANS 1:18 NLT

The hope of the righteous shall be gladness:
but the expectation of the wicked shall perish.

PROVERBS 10:28 KJV

I say to myself, "The LORD is my portion; therefore I will wait
for him." The LORD is good to those whose hope is in him,
to the one who seeks him; it is good to wait
quietly for the salvation of the LORD.

LAMENTATIONS 3:24–26 NIV

There is one body and one Spirit.
There is one hope in which you were called.

EPHESIANS 4:4 NLV

Thou art my hiding place and my shield: I hope in thy word.
PSALM 119:114 KJV

God wants these great riches of the hidden truth to be made
known to the people who are not Jews. The secret is this:
Christ in you brings hope of all the great things to come.
COLOSSIANS 1:27 NLV

Through [Jesus] you believe in God, who raised him
from the dead and glorified him, and so
your faith and hope are in God.
1 PETER 1:21 NIV

Why art thou cast down, O my soul? and why art thou
disquieted within me? hope thou in God: for I shall
yet praise him, who is the health of my
countenance, and my God.
PSALM 42:11 KJV

*What a joy to hope in You, Jesus. I know that all of Your
promises are true, and I anticipate praising You
in heaven throughout eternity. Amen.*

Joy

*God will not force His joy upon you;
you must claim it.*
BETH MOORE

A merry heart doeth good like a medicine.
PROVERBS 17:22 KJV

All the days of the oppressed are wretched,
but the cheerful heart has a continual feast.
PROVERBS 15:15 NIV

So now we can rejoice in our wonderful
new relationship with God because our Lord
Jesus Christ has made us friends of God.
ROMANS 5:11 NLT

"But now I come to You, Father. I say these things
while I am in the world. In this way, My followers
may have My joy in their hearts."
JOHN 17:13 NLV

And the angel said unto them, Fear not:
for, behold, I bring you good tidings of
great joy, which shall be to all people.

LUKE 2:10 KJV

Sorrowful, yet always rejoicing; poor, yet making many rich;
having nothing, and yet possessing everything.

2 CORINTHIANS 6:10 NIV

So rejoice in the LORD and be glad, all you who obey him!
Shout for joy, all you whose hearts are pure!

PSALM 32:11 NLT

For our heart is full of joy in Him,
because we trust in His holy name.

PSALM 33:21 NLV

His lord said unto him, Well done, thou good and faithful
servant: thou hast been faithful over a few things, I will
make thee ruler over many things: enter thou
into the joy of thy lord.
MATTHEW 25:21 KJV

"Until now you have not asked for anything in my name.
Ask and you will receive, and your joy will be complete."
JOHN 16:24 NIV

I am overwhelmed with joy in the LORD my God! For he
has dressed me with the clothing of salvation and draped
me in a robe of righteousness. I am like a bridegroom
dressed for his wedding or a bride with her jewels.
ISAIAH 61:10 NLT

A sinful man is trapped by his sins,
but a man who is right with God sings for joy.
PROVERBS 29:6 NLV

Is anyone happy? Let them sing songs of praise.
JAMES 5:13 NIV

Let all those that seek thee rejoice and be glad
in thee: let such as love thy salvation say
continually, The LORD be magnified.
PSALM 40:16 KJV

Shout for joy to the LORD, all the earth. Worship the LORD
with gladness; come before him with joyful songs.
PSALM 100:1–2 NIV

I will shout for joy and sing your praises,
for you have ransomed me.
PSALM 71:23 NLT

We are not the boss of your faith but we are working
with you to make you happy. Your faith is strong.
2 CORINTHIANS 1:24 NLV

Rejoice in the LORD always: and again I say, Rejoice.
PHILIPPIANS 4:4 KJV

"Blessed are you when people hate you.... Rejoice in that day and leap for joy, because great is your reward in heaven. For that is how their ancestors treated the prophets."

LUKE 6:22–23 NIV

The LORD is my strength and shield. I trust him with all my heart. He helps me, and my heart is filled with joy. I burst out in songs of thanksgiving.

PSALM 28:7 NLT

So the people, for whom the Lord paid the price to be saved, will return. They will come with songs of joy to Zion. Joy that lasts forever will be on their heads. They will receive joy and happiness, and sorrow and sad voices will hurry away.

ISAIAH 51:11 NLV

Lord, allow me see the humor in life. Please don't let me take life too seriously. Remind me to share my happiness with others—when someone needs a smile today, may it be mine. Amen.

Kindness

By showing love through acts of kindness, we can point people toward the God who is both kindness and love.
AMY NAPPA

And he said, Blessed be thou of the LORD, my daughter: for thou hast shewed more kindness in the latter end than at the beginning. . . . And now, my daughter, fear not; I will do to thee all that thou requirest.
RUTH 3:10–11 KJV

"If you let people use your things and expect to get something back, what pay can you expect from that? Even sinners let sinners use things and they expect to get something back. But love those who hate you. Do good to them. Let them use your things and do not expect something back. Your reward will be much. You will be the children of the Most High. He is kind to those who are not thankful and to those who are full of sin."
LUKE 6:34–35 NLV

Supplement. . .godliness with brotherly affection, and
brotherly affection with love for everyone. The more you
grow like this, the more productive and useful you will
be in your knowledge of our Lord Jesus Christ.
2 PETER 1:5, 7–8 NLT

Therefore, as we have opportunity, let us do good to
all people, especially to those who belong to
the family of believers.
GALATIANS 6:10 NIV

But in all things approving ourselves as the ministers
of God. . .by pureness, by knowledge,
by longsuffering, by kindness.
2 CORINTHIANS 6:4, 6 KJV

"Give to any person who asks you for something. If a person
takes something from you, do not ask for it back."
LUKE 6:30 NLV

"Give to the one who asks you, and do not turn away
from the one who wants to borrow from you."
MATTHEW 5:42 NIV

It is a sin to belittle one's neighbor;
blessed are those who help the poor.
PROVERBS 14:21 NLT

Let every one of us please his neighbour
for his good to edification.
ROMANS 15:2 KJV

When someone does something bad to you, do not do
the same thing to him. When someone talks about you,
do not talk about him. Instead, pray that good will
come to him. You were called to do this so you
might receive good things from God.
1 PETER 3:9 NLV

Since God chose you to be the holy people he loves,
you must clothe yourselves with tenderhearted mercy,
kindness, humility, gentleness, and patience.
COLOSSIANS 3:12 NLT

Rejoice with those who rejoice;
mourn with those who mourn.
ROMANS 12:15 NIV

She openeth her mouth with wisdom;
and in her tongue is the law of kindness.
PROVERBS 31:26 KJV

What is desired in a man is his kindness,
and it is better to be a poor man than a liar.
PROVERBS 19:22 NLV

"This is what the LORD of Heaven's Armies says: Judge fairly,
and show mercy and kindness to one another. Do not
oppress widows, orphans, foreigners, and the poor.
And do not scheme against each other."
ZECHARIAH 7:9–10 NLT

*Heavenly Father, please help me to be kind to those around
me today. Change my thoughts. Control my tongue.
Let them see Your love through me. Amen.*

Love for Others

*If I put my own good name before the other's
highest good, then I know nothing of Calvary love.*
AMY CARMICHAEL

A new commandment I give unto you, That ye love one
another; as I have loved you, that ye also love one
another. By this shall all men know that ye are
my disciples, if ye have love one to another.
JOHN 13:34–35 KJV

Let us help each other to love others and to do good.
HEBREWS 10:24 NLV

Three things will last forever—faith, hope,
and love—and the greatest of these is love.
1 CORINTHIANS 13:13 NLT

So this weak brother or sister, for whom Christ died,
is destroyed by your knowledge. When you sin
against them in this way and wound their
weak conscience, you sin against Christ.
1 CORINTHIANS 8:11–12 NIV

As you live God-like,
be kind to Christian brothers and love them.
2 PETER 1:7 NLV

Be kindly affectioned one to another with brotherly love;
in honour preferring one another.
ROMANS 12:10 KJV

Beloved, if God so loved us, we ought also to love one
another. No man hath seen God at any time. If we love one
another, God dwelleth in us, and his love is perfected in us.
1 JOHN 4:11–12 KJV

Dear friends, let us love each other, because love comes from
God. Those who love are God's children and they know God.
Those who do not love do not know God because God is love.
God has shown His love to us by sending His only Son into
the world. God did this so we might have life through Christ.
This is love! It is not that we loved God but that He loved
us. For God sent His Son to pay for our sins with His
own blood. Dear friends, if God loved us that
much, then we should love each other.

1 JOHN 4:7–11 NLV

But we don't need to write to you about the importance
of loving each other, for God himself has
taught you to love one another.
1 Thessalonians 4:9 nlt

For the entire law is fulfilled in keeping this one
command: "Love your neighbor as yourself."
Galatians 5:14 niv

For this is the message that ye heard from the
beginning, that we should love one another.
1 John 3:11 kjv

But anyone who does not love
does not know God, for God is love.
1 John 4:8 nlt

We know what love is because Christ gave His life for us.
We should give our lives for our brothers. What if a person
has enough money to live on and sees his brother in need of
food and clothing? If he does not help him, how can the love
of God be in him? My children, let us not love with words
or in talk only. Let us love by what we do and in truth.
This is how we know we are Christians. It will give our
heart comfort for sure when we stand before Him.
1 John 3:16–19 nlv

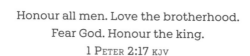

Honour all men. Love the brotherhood.
Fear God. Honour the king.
1 Peter 2:17 kjv

Whoever claims to love God yet hates a brother or sister is
a liar. For whoever does not love their brother and sister,
whom they have seen, cannot love God, whom they have
not seen. And he has given us this command: Anyone who
loves God must also love their brother and sister.
1 John 4:20–21 niv

So now we can tell who are children of God and who are
children of the devil. Anyone who does not live righteously
and does not love other believers does not belong to God.
1 John 3:10 nlt

Let no debt remain outstanding,
except the continuing debt to love one another,
for whoever loves others has fulfilled the law.
Romans 13:8 niv

Seeing ye have purified your souls in obeying the truth through the Spirit unto unfeigned love of the brethren, see that ye love one another with a pure heart fervently.

1 PETER 1:22 KJV

"This is what I tell you to do: Love each other just as I have loved you. No one can have greater love than to give his life for his friends."

JOHN 15:12–13 NLV

"Do not seek revenge or bear a grudge against anyone among your people, but love your neighbor as yourself. I am the LORD."

LEVITICUS 19:18 NIV

If I could speak all the languages of earth and of angels, but didn't love others, I would only be a noisy gong or a clanging cymbal. If I had the gift of prophecy, and if I understood all of God's secret plans and possessed all knowledge, and if I had such faith that I could move mountains, but didn't love others, I would be nothing. If I gave everything I have to the poor and even sacrificed my body, I could boast about it; but if I didn't love others, I would have gained nothing.

1 CORINTHIANS 13:1–3 NLT

Ye have heard that it hath been said, Thou shalt love thy neighbour, and hate thine enemy. But I say unto you, Love your enemies, bless them that curse you, do good to them that hate you, and pray for them which despitefully use you, and persecute you; that ye may be the children of your Father which is in heaven: for he maketh his sun to rise on the evil and on the good, and sendeth rain on the just and on the unjust.

MATTHEW 5:43–45 KJV

Heavenly Father, help me to love others unconditionally. As I'm reminded that You love me in spite of my imperfections, let me extend that same love to those I come in contact with. Amen.

Meekness

One can so easily become too great to be used by God.
One can never be too small for His service.
CORRIE TEN BOOM

Blessed are the meek: for they shall inherit the earth.
MATTHEW 5:5 KJV

Brothers and sisters, if someone is caught in a sin,
you who live by the Spirit should restore that person
gently. But watch yourselves, or you also may be
tempted. Carry each other's burdens, and in
this way you will fulfill the law of Christ.
GALATIANS 6:1–2 NIV

But the meek shall inherit the earth; and shall delight
themselves in the abundance of peace.
PSALM 37:11 KJV

For the LORD delights in his people;
he crowns the humble with victory.
PSALM 149:4 NLT

Good and right is the Lord. So He teaches sinners
in His ways. He leads those without pride into
what is right, and teaches them His way.
PSALM 25:8–9 NLV

Great is our Lord, and of great power:
his understanding is infinite. The LORD lifteth up the
meek: he casteth the wicked down to the ground.
PSALM 147:5–6 KJV

Wives, in the same way submit yourselves to your own
husbands so that, if any of them do not believe the word,
they may be won over without words by the behavior of
their wives. . . . Your beauty should not come from outward
adornment, such as elaborate hairstyles and the wearing
of gold jewelry or fine clothes. Rather, it should be that
of your inner self, the unfading beauty of a gentle and
quiet spirit, which is of great worth in God's sight.
1 PETER 3:1, 3–4 NIV

Look for the Lord, all you people of the earth who are not
proud, and who have obeyed His Laws. Look for what
is right and good. Have no pride. You may be
kept safe on the day of the Lord's anger.

ZEPHANIAH 2:3 NLV

The humble will be filled with fresh joy from the LORD.
The poor will rejoice in the Holy One of Israel.

ISAIAH 29:19 NLT

The meek shall eat and be satisfied: they shall praise the
LORD that seek him: your heart shall live for ever.

PSALM 22:26 KJV

The Spirit of the Sovereign LORD is on me, because the LORD
has anointed me to proclaim good news to the poor. He has
sent me to bind up the brokenhearted, to proclaim freedom
for the captives and release from darkness for the prisoners.

ISAIAH 61:1 NIV

*Lord God, I pray that I will have a spirit of meekness.
Help me to follow Your example, being mild, yet not
weak. For if I can maintain this balance,
I will have strength through You. Amen.*

Mercy

God deals with us from a merciful posture;
His arms are open, His words are healing,
He wants sinners to return to Him.
MARTIE STOWELL

"His mercy extends to those who fear him,
from generation to generation."
LUKE 1:50 NIV

Be ye therefore merciful, as your Father also is merciful.
LUKE 6:36 KJV

We think of those who stayed true to Him as happy even
though they suffered. You have heard how long Job waited.
You have seen what the Lord did for him in the end.
The Lord is full of loving-kindness and pity.
JAMES 5:11 NLV

Blessed are the merciful: for they shall obtain mercy.
MATTHEW 5:7 KJV

All praise to God, the Father of our Lord Jesus Christ.
It is by his great mercy that we have been born again,
because God raised Jesus Christ from the dead.
Now we live with great expectation.

1 PETER 1:3 NLT

But because of his great love for us, God, who is rich in
mercy, made us alive with Christ even when we were dead
in transgressions—it is by grace you have been saved.

EPHESIANS 2:4–5 NIV

But thou, O Lord, art a God full of compassion, and gracious,
long suffering, and plenteous in mercy and truth.

PSALM 86:15 KJV

For God has bound everyone over to disobedience
so that he may have mercy on them all.

ROMANS 11:32 NIV

"I will show loving-kindness to them and forgive their sins.
I will remember their sins no more." When God spoke about a
New Way of Worship, He showed that the Old Way of Worship
was finished and of no use now. It will never be used again.

HEBREWS 8:12–13 NLV

For thou, Lord, art good, and ready to forgive;
and plenteous in mercy unto all them that call upon thee.
PSALM 86:5 KJV

O people, the LORD has told you what is good, and this is
what he requires of you: to do what is right, to love
mercy, and to walk humbly with your God.
MICAH 6:8 NLT

He that covereth his sins shall not prosper: but whoso
confesseth and forsaketh them shall have mercy.
PROVERBS 28:13 KJV

Let the wicked forsake their ways and the unrighteous their
thoughts. Let them turn to the LORD, and he will have mercy
on them, and to our God, for he will freely pardon.
ISAIAH 55:7 NIV

Mercy and truth are met together; righteousness
and peace have kissed each other.
PSALM 85:10 KJV

He saved us, not because of the righteous things we had done, but because of his mercy. He washed away our sins, giving us a new birth and new life through the Holy Spirit. He generously poured out the Spirit upon us through Jesus Christ our Savior. Because of his grace he made us right in his sight and gave us confidence that we will inherit eternal life.

TITUS 3:5–7 NLT

The LORD is good to all: and his tender mercies are over all his works.

PSALM 145:9 KJV

Therefore turn thou to thy God: keep mercy and judgment, and wait on thy God continually.

HOSEA 12:6 KJV

You are a forgiving God, gracious and compassionate, slow to anger and abounding in love.

NEHEMIAH 9:17 NIV

Father, forgive me for keeping record of wrongs others have committed against me. Just as You have forgotten all of my sins and failures, let me show that same mercy to others. Erase the wrongs from my memory, I pray. Amen.

Obedience

In the Bible, power always follows obedience.
SHARON JAYNES

All the ways of the LORD are loving and faithful toward
those who keep the demands of his covenant.
PSALM 25:10 NIV

And Samuel said, Hath the LORD as great delight in burnt
offerings and sacrifices, as in obeying the voice of the
LORD? Behold, to obey is better than sacrifice,
and to hearken than the fat of rams.
1 SAMUEL 15:22 KJV

And this world is fading away, along with everything
that people crave. But anyone who does
what pleases God will live forever.
1 JOHN 2:17 NLT

Happy are those who keep His Law
and look for Him with all their heart.
PSALM 119:2 NLV

But [Jesus] said, Yea rather, blessed are they
that hear the word of God, and keep it.
LUKE 11:28 KJV

But whoever looks intently into the perfect law that gives
freedom, and continues in it—not forgetting what they have
heard, but doing it—they will be blessed in what they do.
JAMES 1:25 NIV

For merely listening to the law doesn't make us right with
God. It is obeying the law that makes us right in his sight.
ROMANS 2:13 NLT

Remember that our fathers on earth punished us.
We had respect for them. How much more should
we obey our Father in heaven and live?
HEBREWS 12:9 NLV

I command thee this day to love the LORD thy God, to walk in
his ways, and to keep his commandments and his statutes
and his judgments, that thou mayest live and multiply:
and the LORD thy God shall bless thee in the
land whither thou goest to possess it.
DEUTERONOMY 30:16 KJV

"If they obey and serve him, they will spend the rest of their days in prosperity and their years in contentment."

JOB 36:11 NIV

"If you will only obey me, you will have plenty to eat."

ISAIAH 1:19 NLT

If ye keep my commandments, ye shall abide in my love; even as I have kept my Father's commandments, and abide in his love.

JOHN 15:10 KJV

Carefully follow the terms of this covenant, so that you may prosper in everything you do.

DEUTERONOMY 29:9 NIV

That's the whole story. Here now is my final conclusion: Fear God and obey his commands, for this is everyone's duty.

ECCLESIASTES 12:13 NLT

My son, do not forget my teaching. Let your heart
keep my words. For they will add to you many
days and years of life and peace.

PROVERBS 3:1–2 NLV

Not every one that saith unto me, Lord, Lord, shall enter
into the kingdom of heaven; but he that doeth
the will of my Father which is in heaven.

MATTHEW 7:21 KJV

Be careful to obey all these regulations I am giving you,
so that it may always go well with you and your children
after you, because you will be doing what is good
and right in the eyes of the LORD your God.

DEUTERONOMY 12:28 NIV

Keep putting into practice all you learned and received
from me—everything you heard from me and saw me
doing. Then the God of peace will be with you.

PHILIPPIANS 4:9 NLT

"Keep His Laws which I am giving you today. Then it may go well with you and your children after you. And you may live long in the land the Lord your God is giving you for all time."

DEUTERONOMY 4:40 NLV

"Therefore anyone who sets aside one of the least of these commands and teaches others accordingly will be called least in the kingdom of heaven, but whoever practices and teaches these commands will be called great in the kingdom of heaven."

MATTHEW 5:19 NIV

Wherefore, my beloved, as ye have always obeyed, not as in my presence only, but now much more in my absence, work out your own salvation with fear and trembling.

PHILIPPIANS 2:12 KJV

Father, the path of life is often difficult. I ask not that You make it smooth, but to illuminate it so that I can see to walk in obedience. If for a moment the light is dim, let me walk by faith, trusting You with each step I take. For Your way is perfect. Amen.

Patience

*The time you spend waiting today can become
the critical time God uses to prepare you
for the answers to your prayers.*
GINGER GARRETT

And let us not be weary in well doing:
for in due season we shall reap, if we faint not.
GALATIANS 6:9 KJV

We glory in tribulations also: knowing that tribulation
worketh patience; and patience, experience;
and experience, hope.
ROMANS 5:3–4 KJV

And so after waiting patiently,
Abraham received what was promised.
HEBREWS 6:15 NIV

May the Lord lead your hearts into a full understanding
and expression of the love of God and the patient
endurance that comes from Christ.
2 THESSALONIANS 3:5 NLT

And the servant of the Lord must not strive;
but be gentle unto all men, apt to teach, patient.
2 Timothy 2:24 KJV

Be patient, then, brothers and sisters, until the Lord's
coming. See how the farmer waits for the land to yield its
valuable crop, patiently waiting for the autumn and
spring rains. You too, be patient and stand firm,
because the Lord's coming is near.
James 5:7–8 NIV

The end of something is better than its beginning.
Not giving up in spirit is better than being proud in
spirit. Do not be quick in spirit to be angry.
For anger is in the heart of fools.
Ecclesiastes 7:8–9 NLV

But in all things approving ourselves as the ministers
of God, in much patience, in afflictions,
in necessities, in distresses.
2 Corinthians 6:4 KJV

"But the seed on good soil stands for those with a noble
and good heart, who hear the word, retain it,
and by persevering produce a crop."
LUKE 8:15 NIV

For what glory is it, if, when ye be buffeted for your faults, ye
shall take it patiently? but if, when ye do well, and suffer for
it, ye take it patiently, this is acceptable with God.
1 PETER 2:20 KJV

Such things were written in the Scriptures long ago
to teach us. And the Scriptures give us hope and
encouragement as we wait patiently for God's promises
to be fulfilled. May God, who gives this patience and
encouragement, help you live in complete harmony with
each other, as is fitting for followers of Christ Jesus.
ROMANS 15:4–5 NLT

For ye have need of patience, that, after ye have done
the will of God, ye might receive the promise.
HEBREWS 10:36 KJV

This calls for patient endurance on the part of the people of God who keep his commands and remain faithful to Jesus.

REVELATION 14:12 NIV

In your patience possess ye your souls.

LUKE 21:19 KJV

For you know that when your faith is tested, your endurance has a chance to grow. So let it grow, for when your endurance is fully developed, you will be perfect and complete, needing nothing.

JAMES 1:3–4 NLT

We ask you, Christian brothers, speak to those who do not want to work. Comfort those who feel they cannot keep going on. Help the weak. Understand and be willing to wait for all men.

1 THESSALONIANS 5:14 NLV

Be still before the LORD and wait patiently for him; do not fret when people succeed in their ways, when they carry out their wicked schemes. Refrain from anger and turn from wrath; do not fret—it leads only to evil. For those who are evil will be destroyed, but those who hope in the LORD will inherit the land.

PSALM 37:7–9 NIV

Be not slothful, but followers of them who through faith
and patience inherit the promises.

HEBREWS 6:12 KJV

To them who by patient continuance in well doing seek
for glory and honour and immortality, eternal life.

ROMANS 2:7 KJV

Wherefore seeing we also are compassed about with so
great a cloud of witnesses, let us lay aside every weight,
and the sin which doth so easily beset us, and let us
run with patience the race that is set before us.

HEBREWS 12:1 KJV

*Lord, sometimes I look for a sign. I want the writing on
the wall or a burning bush experience. I feel like I need
direction, and I need it now! Lord, give me patience.
Give me faith. Instead of seeking a sign, let me live
expectantly for the everyday miracles and
listen for Your still, small voice. Amen.*

Peace

*God's peace can break through
the bleakest of circumstances.*
VIRGINIA ANN FROEHLE

And the fruit of righteousness is sown
in peace of them that make peace.
JAMES 3:18 KJV

The peace of God is much greater than the human
mind can understand. This peace will keep
your hearts and minds through Christ Jesus.
PHILIPPIANS 4:7 NLV

Show them great respect and wholehearted love because
of their work. And live peacefully with each other.
1 THESSALONIANS 5:13 NLT

How good and pleasant it is when
God's people live together in unity!
PSALM 133:1 NIV

Blessed are the peacemakers:
for they shall be called the children of God.
MATTHEW 5:9 KJV

Lying is in the heart of those who plan what is bad,
but those who plan peace have joy.
PROVERBS 12:20 NLV

Make every effort to keep yourselves united in the Spirit,
binding yourselves together with peace.
EPHESIANS 4:3 NLT

Flee the evil desires of youth and pursue righteousness,
faith, love and peace, along with those who
call on the Lord out of a pure heart.
2 TIMOTHY 2:22 NIV

Follow peace with all men, and holiness,
without which no man shall see the Lord.
HEBREWS 12:14 KJV

He will judge between the nations, and will decide for
many people. And they will beat their swords into plows,
and their spears into knives for cutting vines. Nation will
not lift up sword against nation, and they will
not learn about war anymore.

ISAIAH 2:4 NLV

For the Scriptures say, "If you want to enjoy life and see many happy days, keep your tongue from speaking evil and your lips from telling lies. Turn away from evil and do good. Search for peace, and work to maintain it."
1 PETER 3:10–11 NLT

For the mountains shall depart, and the hills be removed; but my kindness shall not depart from thee, neither shall the covenant of my peace be removed, saith the LORD that hath mercy on thee. . . . And all thy children shall be taught of the LORD; and great shall be the peace of thy children.
ISAIAH 54:10, 13 KJV

"Glory to God in the highest heaven, and on earth peace to those on whom his favor rests."
LUKE 2:14 NIV

First of all, I ask you to pray much for all men and to give thanks for them. Pray for kings and all others who are in power over us so we might live quiet God-like lives in peace.
1 TIMOTHY 2:1–2 NLV

Do all that you can to live in peace with everyone.
ROMANS 12:18 NLT

Mark the perfect man, and behold the upright: for the end of that man is peace.
PSALM 37:37 KJV

Our hope comes from God. May He fill you with joy and
peace because of your trust in Him. May your hope
grow stronger by the power of the Holy Spirit.

ROMANS 15:13 NLV

Peace I leave with you, my peace I give unto you:
not as the world giveth, give I unto you. Let not
your heart be troubled, neither let it be afraid.

JOHN 14:27 KJV

The LORD gives strength to his people;
the LORD blesses his people with peace.

PSALM 29:11 NIV

Thou wilt keep him in perfect peace, whose mind is
stayed on thee: because he trusteth in thee.

ISAIAH 26:3 KJV

When a man's ways please the LORD, he maketh even
his enemies to be at peace with him.

PROVERBS 16:7 KJV

*Lord, I often become distracted with the activities of
everyday life. Please give me a calm spirit, and
help me to rest in Your perfect peace. Amen.*

Perseverance

You may have to fight a battle more than once to win it.
MARGARET THATCHER

Confirming the souls of the disciples, and exhorting
them to continue in the faith, and that we must through
much tribulation enter into the kingdom of God.
ACTS 14:22 KJV

For I am convinced that neither death nor life, neither angels
nor demons, neither the present nor the future, nor any
powers, neither height nor depth, nor anything else in all
creation, will be able to separate us from the love
of God that is in Christ Jesus our Lord.
ROMANS 8:38–39 NIV

It gives us new life to know that you
are standing firm in the Lord.
1 THESSALONIANS 3:8 NLT

For this reason, I am suffering. But I am not ashamed.
I know the One in Whom I have put my trust. I am sure
He is able to keep safe that which I have trusted to Him
until the day He comes again. Keep all the things
I taught you. They were given to you in
the faith and love of Jesus Christ.

2 Timothy 1:12–13 nlv

For we are made partakers of Christ, if we hold the
beginning of our confidence stedfast unto the end.

Hebrews 3:14 kjv

He that hath an ear, let him hear what the Spirit saith
unto the churches; He that overcometh shall
not be hurt of the second death.

Revelation 2:11 kjv

Let us hold unswervingly to the hope we profess,
for he who promised is faithful.

Hebrews 10:23 niv

You must pray at all times as the Holy Spirit leads you to
pray. Pray for the things that are needed. You must watch
and keep on praying. Remember to pray for all Christians.

Ephesians 6:18 nlv

So Christ has truly set us free. Now make sure that you stay free, and don't get tied up again in slavery to the law.

GALATIANS 5:1 NLT

Teaching us that, denying ungodliness and worldly lusts, we should live soberly, righteously, and godly, in this present world; looking for that blessed hope, and the glorious appearing of the great God and our Saviour Jesus Christ.

TITUS 2:12–13 KJV

These have come so that the proven genuineness of your faith—of greater worth than gold, which perishes even though refined by fire—may result in praise, glory and honor when Jesus Christ is revealed.

1 PETER 1:7 NIV

Jesus said to the people who believed in him, "You are truly my disciples if you remain faithful to my teachings."

JOHN 8:31 NLT

Keep on staying true to the Lord, my dear friends.

PHILIPPIANS 4:1 NLV

Thou therefore endure hardness,
as a good soldier of Jesus Christ.
2 TIMOTHY 2:3 KJV

Though they stumble, they will never fall,
for the LORD holds them by the hand.
PSALM 37:24 NLT

"To the one who is victorious, I will give the right to
sit with me on my throne, just as I was victorious
and sat down with my Father on his throne."
REVELATION 3:21 NIV

Therefore, since we are surrounded by such a great cloud
of witnesses, let us throw off everything that hinders
and the sin that so easily entangles. And let us run with
perseverance the race marked out for us, fixing our eyes
on Jesus, the pioneer and perfecter of faith. For the joy set
before him he endured the cross, scorning its shame,
and sat down at the right hand of the throne of God.
HEBREWS 12:1–2 NIV

Wherefore take unto you the whole armour of God,
that ye may be able to withstand in the evil
day, and having done all, to stand.

EPHESIANS 6:13 KJV

Can anything ever separate us from Christ's love?
Does it mean he no longer loves us if we have
trouble or calamity, or are persecuted, or hungry,
or destitute, or in danger, or threatened with death?

ROMANS 8:35 NLT

Ye therefore, beloved, seeing ye know these things before,
beware lest ye also, being led away with the error of
the wicked, fall from your own stedfastness.

2 PETER 3:17 KJV

*Father, sometimes I get so weary and want to give up.
But You have promised a life of blessing if I
will persevere. Thank You for giving me the
strength I need to "run the race." Amen.*

Prayer

Fretting magnifies the problem,
but prayer magnifies God.
JOANNA WEAVER

But we will give ourselves continually to prayer,
and to the ministry of the word.
ACTS 6:4 KJV

"In that day you will no longer ask me anything.
Very truly I tell you, my Father will give you whatever
you ask in my name. Until now you have not asked for
anything in my name. Ask and you will receive,
and your joy will be complete."
JOHN 16:23–24 NIV

"When you pray, go into a room by yourself. After you have
shut the door, pray to your Father Who is in secret. Then your
Father Who sees in secret will reward you. When you pray,
do not say the same thing over and over again making long
prayers like the people who do not know God. They think
they are heard because their prayers are long."
MATTHEW 6:6–7 NLV

O Lord, hear me as I pray; pay attention to my groaning.
Listen to my cry for help, my King and my God, for I pray
to no one but you. Listen to my voice in the morning,
Lord. Each morning I bring my requests
to you and wait expectantly.
PSALM 5:1–3 NLT

Rejoicing in hope; patient in tribulation;
continuing instant in prayer.
ROMANS 12:12 KJV

Evening, morning and noon I cry out
in distress, and he hears my voice.
PSALM 55:17 NIV

"You are bad and you know how to give good things to your
children. How much more will your Father in heaven
give good things to those who ask Him?"
MATTHEW 7:11 NLV

He will be gracious if you ask for help.
He will surely respond to the sound of your cries.
ISAIAH 30:19 NLT

Pray without ceasing.
1 THESSALONIANS 5:17 KJV

"You will pray to him, and he will hear you,
and you will fulfill your vows."
JOB 22:27 NIV

You must pray at all times as the Holy Spirit leads you to
pray. Pray for the things that are needed. You must watch
and keep on praying. Remember to pray for all Christians.
EPHESIANS 6:18 NLV

I waited patiently for the LORD to help me,
and he turned to me and heard my cry.
PSALM 40:1 NLT

And shall not God avenge his own elect, which cry day
and night unto him, though he bear long with them?
LUKE 18:7 KJV

"If you believe, you will receive
whatever you ask for in prayer."
MATTHEW 21:22 NIV

"If My people who are called by My name put away their
pride and pray, and look for My face, and turn from
their sinful ways, then I will hear from heaven.
I will forgive their sin, and will heal their land."
2 CHRONICLES 7:14 NLV

"In those days when you pray, I will listen.
If you look for me wholeheartedly, you will find me. "
JEREMIAH 29:12–13 NLT

The LORD is nigh unto all them that call upon him,
to all that call upon him in truth.
PSALM 145:18 KJV

Let us then approach God's throne of grace with
confidence, so that we may receive mercy and
find grace to help us in our time of need.
HEBREWS 4:16 NIV

The Lord hates the gifts of the sinful,
but the prayer of the faithful is His joy.
PROVERBS 15:8 NLV

"Keep on asking, and you will receive what you ask for.
Keep on seeking, and you will find. Keep on knocking,
and the door will be opened to you. For everyone who
asks, receives. Everyone who seeks, finds. And to
everyone who knocks, the door will be opened."
MATTHEW 7:7–8 NLT

And it shall come to pass, that before they call,
I will answer; and while they are yet speaking, I will hear.
ISAIAH 65:24 KJV

Therefore confess your sins to each other and pray for
each other so that you may be healed. The prayer
of a righteous person is powerful and effective.
JAMES 5:16 NIV

We are sure that if we ask anything that He wants us to have,
He will hear us. If we are sure He hears us when we ask, we
can be sure He will give us what we ask for.
1 JOHN 5:14–15 NLV

And the Holy Spirit helps us in our weakness. For example,
we don't know what God wants us to pray for. But the
Holy Spirit prays for us with groanings that
cannot be expressed in words.
ROMANS 8:26 NLT

I will therefore that men pray every where,
lifting up holy hands, without wrath and doubting.
1 TIMOTHY 2:8 KJV

I will pray with my spirit, but I will also pray with
my understanding; I will sing with my spirit,
but I will also sing with my understanding.
1 Corinthians 14:15 niv

Do not worry. Learn to pray about everything. Give thanks
to God as you ask Him for what you need. The peace of God
is much greater than the human mind can understand. This
peace will keep your hearts and minds through Christ Jesus.
Philippians 4:6–7 nlv

But each day the Lord pours his unfailing love upon me,
and through each night I sing his songs,
praying to God who gives me life.
Psalm 42:8 nlt

Again I say unto you, That if two of you shall agree on earth as
touching any thing that they shall ask, it shall be done for them
of my Father which is in heaven. For where two or three are
gathered together in my name, there am I in the midst of them.
Matthew 18:19–20 kjv

"He will call on me, and I will answer him; I will be with him in trouble, I will deliver him and honor him."
PSALM 91:15 NIV

I will call on Him as long as I live,
because He has turned His ear to me.
PSALM 116:2 NLV

Are any of you suffering hardships? You should pray. Are any of you happy? You should sing praises. Are any of you sick? You should call for the elders of the church to come and pray over you, anointing you with oil in the name of the Lord. Such a prayer offered in faith will heal the sick, and the Lord will make you well. And if you have committed any sins, you will be forgiven.
JAMES 5:13–15 NLT

Dear God, I pray for my friends and family. Please protect them and help them to grow closer to You each day. I pray this for myself, also, Lord. I want to communicate with You continually, sharing from my heart, then quietly and patiently waiting for Your voice. Thank You, Father, for listening to my prayer. Amen.

Protection

No storm is so great, no wave is so high, no sea is so deep, no wind is so strong, that Jesus cannot either calm it or carry us through it.
ANNE GRAHAM LOTZ

Above all, taking the shield of faith, wherewith ye shall be able to quench all the fiery darts of the wicked.
EPHESIANS 6:16 KJV

"The LORD is my rock, my fortress, and my savior; my God is my rock, in whom I find protection. He is my shield, the power that saves me, and my place of safety. He is my refuge, my savior, the one who saves me from violence. I called on the LORD, who is worthy of praise, and he saved me from my enemies."
2 SAMUEL 22:2–4 NLT

Be my rock of refuge, to which I can always go; give the command to save me, for you are my rock and my fortress.
PSALM 71:3 NIV

But the Lord has been my strong place,
my God, and the rock where I am safe.
PSALM 94:22 NLV

But whoso hearkeneth unto me shall dwell safely,
and shall be quiet from fear of evil.
PROVERBS 1:33 KJV

Give your burdens to the LORD, and he will take care of you.
He will not permit the godly to slip and fall.
PSALM 55:22 NLT

"Every word of God is flawless; he is a shield to
those who take refuge in him."
PROVERBS 30:5 NIV

For You are my rock and my safe place. For the honor
of Your name, lead me and show me the way.
PSALM 31:3 NLV

For thou, LORD, wilt bless the righteous;
with favour wilt thou compass him as with a shield.
PSALM 5:12 KJV

God is our refuge and strength,
always ready to help in times of trouble.
PSALM 46:1 NLT

God is our refuge and strength, an ever-present help
in trouble. Therefore we will not fear, though the earth
give way and the mountains fall into the heart of
the sea, though its waters roar and foam and
the mountains quake with their surging.
PSALM 46:1–3 NIV

He will cover you with his feathers. He will shelter
you with his wings. His faithful promises
are your armor and protection.
PSALM 91:4 NLT

In the fear of the LORD is strong confidence:
and his children shall have a place of refuge.
PROVERBS 14:26 KJV

Our soul waits for the Lord.
He is our help and our safe cover.
PSALM 33:20 NLV

"The eternal God is your refuge,
and his everlasting arms are under you."
Deuteronomy 33:27 NLT

The Lord is a refuge for the oppressed,
a stronghold in times of trouble.
Psalm 9:9 NIV

The Lord is good, a strong hold in the day of trouble;
and he knoweth them that trust in him.
Nahum 1:7 KJV

The Lord is my rock, my fortress, and my savior; my God is
my rock, in whom I find protection. He is my shield,
the power that saves me, and my place of safety.
Psalm 18:2 NLT

"The Lord lives. Thanks be to my Rock.
May God be honored, the Rock that saves me."
2 Samuel 22:47 NLV

The Lord Almighty is with us;
the God of Jacob is our fortress.
Psalm 46:7 NIV

The name of the LORD is a strong fortress;
the godly run to him and are safe.
PROVERBS 18:10 NLT

You have also given me the covering that saves me. Your
right hand holds me up. And Your care has made me great.
PSALM 18:35 NLV

When thou passest through the waters, I will be with
thee; and through the rivers, they shall not overflow thee:
when thou walkest through the fire, thou shalt not be
burned; neither shall the flame kindle upon thee.

ISAIAH 43:2 KJV

*Dear Father, thank You for Your physical protection as
well as spiritual protection. There are so many
occasions when I could falter, but You guard my
feet. I trust You to protect me today. Amen.*

Purity

*The only thing that tarnishes us is our own sin,
and we are one simple prayer of repentance
away from purity at all times.*
BETH MOORE

It is God's will that you should be sanctified:
that you should avoid sexual immorality.
1 THESSALONIANS 4:3 NIV

Drink waters out of thine own cistern,
and running waters out of thine own well.
PROVERBS 5:15 KJV

So put to death the sinful, earthly things lurking within you.
Have nothing to do with sexual immorality, impurity, lust,
and evil desires. Don't be greedy, for a greedy person is an
idolater, worshiping the things of this world. Because of
these sins, the anger of God is coming.
COLOSSIANS 3:5–6 NLT

Do not let sex sins or anything sinful be even talked
about among those who belong to Christ.
Do not always want everything.
EPHESIANS 5:3 NLV

Thou shalt not commit adultery.
EXODUS 20:14 KJV

I also want the women to dress modestly, with decency
and propriety, adorning themselves, not with elaborate
hairstyles or gold or pearls or expensive clothes,
but with good deeds, appropriate for women
who profess to worship God.
1 TIMOTHY 2:9–10 NIV

*Lord Jesus, my thoughts and actions are impure at
times. Please renew my mind. Thank You for promising to
forgive me and consider me as white as snow. Amen.*

Repentance

The only way we can walk in the light is to live in a state of continual repentance. It is the cornerstone of the Christian faith.
DEE BRESTIN AND KATHY TROCCOLI

And the times of this ignorance God winked at; but now commandeth all men every where to repent.
ACTS 17:30 KJV

Come near to God and he will come near to you. Wash your hands, you sinners, and purify your hearts, you double-minded.
JAMES 4:8 NIV

People who conceal their sins will not prosper, but if they confess and turn from them, they will receive mercy.
PROVERBS 28:13 NLT

I will have mercy, and not sacrifice: for I am not come to call the righteous, but sinners to repentance.
MATTHEW 9:13 KJV

"I tell you, it is the same way among the angels of God.
If one sinner is sorry for his sins and turns from
them, the angels are very happy."

LUKE 15:10 NLV

Or do you show contempt for the riches of his kindness,
forbearance and patience, not realizing that God's
kindness is intended to lead you to repentance?

ROMANS 2:4 NIV

"Go back to what you heard and believed at first; hold to it
firmly. Repent and turn to me again. If you don't wake up,
I will come to you suddenly, as unexpected as a thief."

REVELATION 3:3 NLT

Repent therefore of this thy wickedness, and pray God,
if perhaps the thought of thine heart may be forgiven thee.

ACTS 8:22 KJV

"Repent, then, and turn to God, so that your sins may be
wiped out, that times of refreshing may come from the Lord."

ACTS 3:19 NIV

The Lord is near to those who have a broken heart.
And He saves those who are broken in spirit.

PSALM 34:18 NLV

Seek the LORD while you can find him. Call on him now while he is near. Let the wicked change their ways and banish the very thought of doing wrong. Let them turn to the LORD that he may have mercy on them. Yes, turn to our God, for he will forgive generously.

ISAIAH 55:6–7 NLT

The Lord is not slack concerning his promise, as some men count slackness; but is longsuffering to us-ward, not willing that any should perish, but that all should come to repentance.

2 PETER 3:9 KJV

"The time has come," he said. "The kingdom of God has come near. Repent and believe the good news!"

MARK 1:15 NIV

Return to the LORD your God, for he is merciful and compassionate, slow to get angry and filled with unfailing love. He is eager to relent and not punish.

JOEL 2:13 NLT

*Father, I come to You to repent of my sins.
Change my heart and my desires, Lord,
so that from this day on I leave
my sins in the past. Amen.*

Rest

Rest communicates something basic about our relationship with God, and God's relationship with us.
JANE RUBIETTA

For he spake in a certain place of the seventh day on this
wise, And God did rest the seventh day from all his works....
There remaineth therefore a rest to the people of God.
HEBREWS 4:4, 9 KJV

Whoever dwells in the shelter of the Most High
will rest in the shadow of the Almighty.
PSALM 91:1 NIV

In peace I will lie down and sleep, for you alone,
O LORD, will keep me safe.
PSALM 4:8 NLT

"Then you would trust, because there is hope.
You would look around and rest and be safe."
JOB 11:18 NLV

It is vain for you to rise up early, to sit up late, to eat the
bread of sorrows: for so he giveth his beloved sleep.
PSALM 127:2 KJV

Rest in the Lord and be willing to wait for Him.
Do not trouble yourself when all goes well with
the one who carries out his sinful plans.
PSALM 37:7 NLV

"You have six days each week for your ordinary work,
but the seventh day must be a Sabbath day of complete
rest, a holy day dedicated to the LORD."
EXODUS 31:15 NLT

When thou liest down, thou shalt not be afraid: yea, thou
shalt lie down, and thy sleep shall be sweet.
PROVERBS 3:24 KJV

*Slow me down, Lord. My schedule gets so hectic that I find
myself with my priorities in the wrong order. Grant me a
few moments of quiet, so that I may collect my
thoughts and be refreshed. Amen.*

Righteousness

*Even though we still sin and often can't seem
to stop, God declared us righteous when
we believed and received Jesus.*
PATSY CLAIRMONT AND TRACI MULLINS

Blessed are they which do hunger and thirst after
righteousness: for they shall be filled.
MATTHEW 5:6 KJV

"Blessed are those who are persecuted because of
righteousness, for theirs is the kingdom of heaven."
MATTHEW 5:10 NIV

"But if you are careful to obey him, following all my
instructions, then I will be an enemy to your enemies,
and I will oppose those who oppose you."
EXODUS 23:22 NLT

Know that the Lord has set apart him who is God-like
for Himself. The Lord hears when I call to Him.
PSALM 4:3 NLV

A righteous man hateth lying: but a wicked man
is loathsome, and cometh to shame.
PROVERBS 13:5 KJV

"But seek first his kingdom and his righteousness,
and all these things will be given to you as well."
MATTHEW 6:33 NIV

"If you fully obey the LORD your God and carefully keep all
his commands that I am giving you today, the LORD your
God will set you high above all the nations of the world."
DEUTERONOMY 28:1 NLT

He who follows what is right and loving and kind
finds life, right-standing with God and honor.
PROVERBS 21:21 NLV

He withdraweth not his eyes from the righteous:
but with kings are they on the throne; yea, he doth
establish them for ever, and they are exalted.
JOB 36:7 KJV

If we confess our sins, he is faithful and just and will forgive
us our sins and purify us from all unrighteousness.
1 JOHN 1:9 NIV

Don't you realize that those who do wrong will not inherit
the Kingdom of God? Don't fool yourselves.

1 Corinthians 6:9 nlt

O Lord, who may live in Your tent? Who may live on Your holy
hill? He who walks without blame and does what is right
and good, and speaks the truth in his heart.

Psalm 15:1–2 nlv

The eyes of the Lord are upon the righteous,
and his ears are open unto their cry.

Psalm 34:15 kjv

The Lord does not let the righteous go hungry,
but he thwarts the craving of the wicked.

Proverbs 10:3 niv

The Lord hears his people when they call to him for help.
He rescues them from all their troubles.

Psalm 34:17 nlt

The man who is right and good will be glad in the Lord
and go to Him to be safe. All those whose
hearts are right will give Him praise.

Psalm 64:10 nlv

Then shall he answer them, saying, Verily I say unto you, Inasmuch as ye did it not to one of the least of these, ye did it not to me. And these shall go away into everlasting punishment: but the righteous into life eternal.

MATTHEW 25:45–46 KJV

"Then the righteous will shine like the sun in the kingdom of their Father. Whoever has ears, let them hear."

MATTHEW 13:43 NIV

"Then your salvation will come like the dawn, and your wounds will quickly heal. Your godliness will lead you forward, and the glory of the LORD will protect you from behind."

ISAIAH 58:8 NLT

Let those who love the Lord hate what is bad. For He keeps safe the souls of His faithful ones. He takes them away from the hand of the sinful. Light is spread like seed for those who are right and good, and joy for the pure in heart.

PSALM 97:10–11 NLV

Dear God, I want to seek after Your righteousness, following what is eternal and true. Thank You for Your faithfulness in the times that I seek to do right, even when I must stand alone. Amen.

Salvation

*God's salvation is not a purchase to be made, nor wages
to be earned, nor a summit to be climbed, nor a task
to be accomplished; but it is simply and
only a gift to be accepted.*
HANNAH WHITALL SMITH

But after that the kindness and love of God our Saviour
toward man appeared, not by works of righteousness which
we have done, but according to his mercy he saved us,
by the washing of regeneration, and renewing of the
Holy Ghost; which he shed on us abundantly
through Jesus Christ our Saviour.
TITUS 3:4–6 KJV

Yet to all who did receive him, to those who believed in
his name, he gave the right to become children of God—
children born not of natural descent, nor of human
decision or a husband's will, but born of God.
JOHN 1:12–13 NIV

I, too, try to please everyone in everything I do. I don't
just do what is best for me; I do what is best for
others so that many may be saved.
1 CORINTHIANS 10:33 NLT

Christ never sinned but God put our sin on Him. Then we are made right with God because of what Christ has done for us.

2 CORINTHIANS 5:21 NLV

For this is good and acceptable in the sight of God our Saviour; who will have all men to be saved, and to come unto the knowledge of the truth.

1 TIMOTHY 2:3–4 KJV

"Whoever believes in the Son has eternal life."

JOHN 3:36 NIV

Jesus replied, "I tell you the truth, unless you are born again, you cannot see the Kingdom of God." "What do you mean?" exclaimed Nicodemus. "How can an old man go back into his mother's womb and be born again?" Jesus replied, "I assure you, no one can enter the Kingdom of God without being born of water and the Spirit. Humans can reproduce only human life, but the Holy Spirit gives birth to spiritual life. So don't be surprised when I say, 'You must be born again.' "

JOHN 3:3–7 NLT

My dear children, I am writing this to you so you will not sin. But if anyone does sin, there is One Who will go between him and the Father. He is Jesus Christ, the One Who is right with God. He paid for our sins with His own blood. He did not pay for ours only, but for the sins of the whole world.

1 John 2:1–2 nlv

Neither is there salvation in any other: for there is none other name under heaven given among men, whereby we must be saved.

Acts 4:12 kjv

Therefore, if anyone is in Christ, the new creation has come: The old has gone, the new is here!

2 Corinthians 5:17 niv

Lord, what a sacrifice You made in sending Your only Son to die for me! It should have been me sentenced to that horrible death, but You saved me from the punishment that I deserve. Thank You for the free gift of salvation. Amen.

Scripture

*People who say the Bible isn't relevant
today obviously don't know the Author.*
STORMIE OMARTIAN

For the word of God is quick, and powerful, and sharper than
any twoedged sword, piercing even to the dividing asunder
of soul and spirit, and of the joints and marrow, and is a
discerner of the thoughts and intents of the heart.
HEBREWS 4:12 KJV

Let the message about Christ, in all its richness, fill your
lives. Teach and counsel each other with all the wisdom
he gives. Sing psalms and hymns and spiritual
songs to God with thankful hearts.
COLOSSIANS 3:16 NLT

You have known the Holy Writings since you were a child.
They are able to give you wisdom that leads to being
saved from the punishment of sin by putting
your trust in Christ Jesus.
2 TIMOTHY 3:15 NLV

Concerning this salvation, the prophets, who spoke of
the grace that was to come to you, searched intently and
with the greatest care, trying to find out the time and
circumstances to which the Spirit of Christ in them was
pointing when he predicted the sufferings of the Messiah
and the glories that would follow. It was revealed to them
that they were not serving themselves but you, when they
spoke of the things that have now been told you by those
who have preached the gospel to you by the Holy Spirit sent
from heaven. Even angels long to look into these things.

1 PETER 1:10–12 NIV

It is the same with my word. I send it out, and it always
produces fruit. It will accomplish all I want it to,
and it will prosper everywhere I send it.

ISAIAH 55:11 NLT

You should remember the words that were spoken before
by the holy early preachers. Do not forget the teaching
of the Lord, the One Who saves. This was given
to you by your missionaries.

2 PETER 3:2 NLV

"Keep this Book of the Law always on your lips; meditate on
it day and night, so that you may be careful to do everything
written in it. Then you will be prosperous and successful."

JOSHUA 1:8 NIV

Therefore shall ye lay up these my words in your heart and in your soul, and bind them for a sign upon your hand, that they may be as frontlets between your eyes. And ye shall teach them your children, speaking of them when thou sittest in thine house, and when thou walkest by the way, when thou liest down, and when thou risest up.

DEUTERONOMY 11:18–19 KJV

Thy word have I hid in mine heart,
that I might not sin against thee.

PSALM 119:11 KJV

In the past God spoke to our ancestors through the prophets at many times and in various ways, but in these last days he has spoken to us by his Son, whom he appointed heir of all things, and through whom also he made the universe.

HEBREWS 1:1–2 NIV

Thy word is a lamp unto my feet, and a light unto my path.

PSALM 119:105 KJV

Heavenly Father, I want to hide Your Word in my heart. Give me a clear mind as I meditate on scripture and memorize verses. I want to have Your Truth in the forefront of my mind, so that when I am faced with temptation or adversity, I can refute it with scripture as You did. Thank You for the joy that fills my heart as I reflect on Your Word. Amen.

Seeking God

All over the world, people go to unimaginable lengths
to find God—which is sad when you consider the
unimaginable lengths God has already gone to find us.
JOANNA WEAVER

And ye shall seek me, and find me,
when ye shall search for me with all your heart.
JEREMIAH 29:13 KJV

But if from there you seek the LORD your God, you will find
him if you seek him with all your heart and with all your soul.
DEUTERONOMY 4:29 NIV

"Seek the Kingdom of God above all else,
and he will give you everything you need."
LUKE 12:31 NLT

But seek ye first the kingdom of God, and his righteousness;
and all these things shall be added unto you.
MATTHEW 6:33 KJV

"I say to you, ask, and what you ask for will be given to you.
Look, and what you are looking for you will find. Knock,
and the door you are knocking on will be opened to you."
LUKE 11:9 NLV

Glory in his holy name; let the hearts
of those who seek the LORD rejoice.
1 CHRONICLES 16:10 NIV

If my people, which are called by my name, shall humble
themselves, and pray, and seek my face, and turn from their
wicked ways; then will I hear from heaven, and will
forgive their sin, and will heal their land.
2 CHRONICLES 7:14 KJV

Since you have been raised to new life with Christ, set your
sights on the realities of heaven, where Christ sits
in the place of honor at God's right hand.
COLOSSIANS 3:1 NLT

One thing I have asked from the Lord, that I will look for:
that I may live in the house of the Lord all the days of
my life, to look upon the beauty of the Lord,
and to worship in His holy house.
PSALM 27:4 NLV

Look to the LORD and his strength; seek his face always.

1 CHRONICLES 16:11 NIV

Seek the LORD, and ye shall live.

AMOS 5:6 KJV

"I said, 'Plant the good seeds of righteousness, and you
will harvest a crop of love. Plow up the hard ground of your
hearts, for now is the time to seek the LORD, that he may
come and shower righteousness upon you.' "

HOSEA 10:12 NLT

They that seek the LORD shall not want any good thing.

PSALM 34:10 KJV

My soul yearns for you in the night;
in the morning my spirit longs for you.

ISAIAH 26:9 NIV

*Lord Jesus, I want to have a growing, vital relationship
with You. Please don't let me fall into the complacency of
having a stagnant relationship with You. I will only deepen
my relationships with You and with others when I invest
my time. Thank You for allowing me to come into
Your presence and meditate on You. Amen.*

Self-Control

Your main concern lies in dwelling continually upon the God who is within you. Then, without particularly thinking of self-denial or "putting away the deeds of the flesh," God will cause you to experience a natural subduing of the flesh!
JEANNE GUYON

For this very reason, make every effort to add to your faith goodness; and to goodness, knowledge; and to knowledge, self-control; and to self-control, perseverance; and to perseverance, godliness.
2 PETER 1:5–6 NIV

And every man that striveth for the mastery is temperate in all things. Now they do it to obtain a corruptible crown; but we an incorruptible.
1 CORINTHIANS 9:25 KJV

I discipline my body like an athlete, training it to do what it should. Otherwise, I fear that after preaching to others I myself might be disqualified.
1 CORINTHIANS 9:27 NLT

Love does not give up. Love is kind. Love is not jealous.
Love does not put itself up as being important. Love has
no pride. Love does not do the wrong thing.
Love never thinks of itself.

1 CORINTHIANS 13:4–5 NLV

For even hereunto were ye called: because Christ also
suffered for us, leaving us an example, that ye should follow
his steps: Who did no sin, neither was guile found in his
mouth: Who, when he was reviled, reviled not again;
when he suffered, he threatened not; but committed
himself to him that judgeth righteously.

1 PETER 2:21–23 KJV

For if you live according to the flesh, you will die;
but if by the Spirit you put to death the
misdeeds of the body, you will live.

ROMANS 8:13 NIV

Do you like honey? Don't eat too much,
or it will make you sick!
Proverbs 25:16 nlt

Church helpers must also be good men and act so people
will respect them. They must speak the truth. They must
not get drunk. They must not have a love for money.
1 Timothy 3:8 nlv

Teach the older men to exercise self-control, to be worthy
of respect, and to live wisely. They must have sound
faith and be filled with love and patience.
Titus 2:2 nlt

He sitteth alone and keepeth silence, because he hath
borne it upon him. He putteth his mouth in the
dust; if so be there may be hope.
Lamentations 3:28–29 kjv

Let us behave decently, as in the daytime, not in carousing
and drunkenness, not in sexual immorality and debauchery,
not in dissension and jealousy. Rather, clothe yourselves
with the Lord Jesus Christ, and do not think about
how to gratify the desires of the flesh.
ROMANS 13:13–14 NIV

Neither fornicators, nor idolaters, nor adulterers,
nor effeminate, nor abusers of themselves with mankind,
nor thieves, nor covetous, nor drunkards, nor revilers, nor
extortioners, shall inherit the kingdom of God. And such
were some of you: but ye are washed, but ye are
sanctified, but ye are justified in the name of the
Lord Jesus, and by the Spirit of our God.
1 CORINTHIANS 6:9–11 KJV

Let all people see how gentle you are.
The Lord is coming again soon.
PHILIPPIANS 4:5 NLV

For the grace of God has appeared that offers salvation to
all people. It teaches us to say "No" to ungodliness and
worldly passions, and to live self-controlled,
upright and godly lives in this present age.
TITUS 2:11–12 NIV

Then Pilate said to Him, "Do You not hear all these things they are saying against You?" Jesus did not say a word. The leader was much surprised and wondered about it.

MATTHEW 27:13–14 NLV

Yet Michael the archangel, when contending with the devil he disputed about the body of Moses, durst not bring against him a railing accusation, but said, The Lord rebuke thee.

JUDE 9 KJV

So be on your guard, not asleep like the others. Stay alert and be clearheaded.

1 THESSALONIANS 5:6 NLT

Dear God, I need You to help me resist going along with the crowd when they do things that would displease You. Let my words and actions be a constant beacon, drawing the lost to You. Amen.

Sin

No sin, no matter how momentarily pleasurable, comforting, or habitual, is worth missing what God has for us.
BETH MOORE

He was wounded for our transgressions, he was bruised for our iniquities: the chastisement of our peace was upon him; and with his stripes we are healed. All we like sheep have gone astray; we have turned every one to his own way; and the LORD hath laid on him the iniquity of us all.
ISAIAH 53:5–6 KJV

If we live in the light as He is in the light, we share what we have in God with each other. And the blood of Jesus Christ, His Son, makes our lives clean from all sin.
1 JOHN 1:7 NLV

As far as the east is from the west, so far has he removed our transgressions from us.
PSALM 103:12 NIV

"Come now, let's settle this," says the LORD. "Though your sins are like scarlet, I will make them as white as snow. Though they are red like crimson, I will make them as white as wool."
ISAIAH 1:18 NLT

For I will be merciful to their unrighteousness, and their sins and their iniquities will I remember no more.
HEBREWS 8:12 KJV

"This is My blood of the New Way of Worship which is given for many. It is given so the sins of many can be forgiven."
MATTHEW 26:28 NLV

For we know that our old self was crucified with him so that the body ruled by sin might be done away with, that we should no longer be slaves to sin—because anyone who has died has been set free from sin.
ROMANS 6:6–7 NIV

My dear children, I am writing this to you so that you will not sin. But if anyone does sin, we have an advocate who pleads our case before the Father. He is Jesus Christ, the one who is truly righteous. He himself is the sacrifice that atones for our sins—and not only our sins but the sins of all the world.

1 JOHN 2:1–2 NLT

This is a faithful saying, and worthy of all acceptation,
that Christ Jesus came into the world to
save sinners; of whom I am chief.

1 TIMOTHY 1:15 KJV

"All the early preachers spoke of this. Everyone who puts his
trust in Christ will have his sins forgiven through His name."

ACTS 10:43 NLV

Grace and peace to you from God our Father and the Lord
Jesus Christ, who gave himself for our sins to rescue us
from the present evil age, according to the
will of our God and Father.

GALATIANS 1:3–4 NIV

He personally carried our sins in his body on the cross
so that we can be dead to sin and live for what
is right. By his wounds you are healed.

1 PETER 2:24 NLT

*Lord Jesus, I ask forgiveness for the sins that I've
committed, even today. I repent of them now, asking You to
help me leave them in the past. Nothing is worth separating
me from You. I pray that You will give me the strength
to defeat Satan and his attempts to keep me
from living a life of victory. Amen.*

Strength

There is strength in being weak—God's strength!
Let God step in and do what you cannot.
BARB ALBERT

And he said unto me, My grace is sufficient for
thee: for my strength is made perfect in weakness.
Most gladly therefore will I rather glory in my infirmities,
that the power of Christ may rest upon me.
2 CORINTHIANS 12:9 KJV

Wealth and honor come from you; you are the ruler of
all things. In your hands are strength and power
to exalt and give strength to all.
1 CHRONICLES 29:12 NIV

But they who wait upon the Lord will get new strength.
They will rise up with wings like eagles. They will run and
not get tired. They will walk and not become weak.

ISAIAH 40:31 NLV

"For the eyes of the LORD range throughout the earth to strengthen those whose hearts are fully committed to him."

2 CHRONICLES 16:9 NIV

We prove ourselves by our purity, our understanding, our patience, our kindness, by the Holy Spirit within us, and by our sincere love. We faithfully preach the truth. God's power is working in us. We use the weapons of righteousness in the right hand for attack and the left hand for defense.

2 CORINTHIANS 6:6–7 NLT

Finally, my brethren, be strong in the Lord, and in the power of his might.

EPHESIANS 6:10 KJV

He gives strength to the weary and increases the power of the weak.

ISAIAH 40:29 NIV

I know how to get along with little and how to live when I
have much. I have learned the secret of being happy at all
times. If I am full of food and have all I need, I am happy.
If I am hungry and need more, I am happy. I can do
all things because Christ gives me the strength.

PHILIPPIANS 4:12–13 NLV

My flesh and my heart faileth: but God is the strength
of my heart, and my portion for ever.

PSALM 73:26 KJV

You, God, are awesome in your sanctuary; the God of
Israel gives power and strength to his people.

PSALM 68:35 NIV

I pray that God's great power will make you strong,
and that you will have joy as you wait and do not give up.

COLOSSIANS 1:11 NLV

The Lord is my rock, and my fortress, and my deliverer;
my God, my strength, in whom I will trust; my buckler
and the horn of my salvation, and my high tower.

PSALM 18:2 KJV

The Lord gives his people strength.
The Lord blesses them with peace.

PSALM 29:11 NLT

"The righteous will hold to their ways,
and those with clean hands will grow stronger."

JOB 17:9 NIV

Wait on the Lord: be of good courage, and he shall
strengthen thine heart: wait, I say, on the Lord.

PSALM 27:14 KJV

*Father, help me to see today how I can be useful.
Then give me the strength to walk into the
opportunities You have set before me. Amen.*

Temptation

Nothing so cultivates the grace
as the endurance of temptation.
HANNAH WHITALL SMITH

Lead us not into temptation, but deliver us from evil:
For thine is the kingdom, and the power,
and the glory, for ever. Amen.
MATTHEW 6:13 KJV

On reaching the place, [Jesus] said to them,
"Pray that you will not fall into temptation."
LUKE 22:40 NIV

"Because you have obeyed my command to persevere,
I will protect you from the great time of testing that
will come upon the whole world to test
those who belong to this world."
REVELATION 3:10 NLT

Blessed is the man that endureth temptation: for when he
is tried, he shall receive the crown of life, which the
Lord hath promised to them that love him.

JAMES 1:12 KJV

When you are tempted to do wrong, do not say,
"God is tempting me." God cannot be tempted.
He will never tempt anyone.
JAMES 1:13 NLV

The Lord knoweth how to deliver the
godly out of temptations.
2 PETER 2:9 KJV

You have never been tempted to sin in any different way
than other people. God is faithful. He will not allow you to be
tempted more than you can take. But when you are tempted,
He will make a way for you to keep from falling into sin.
1 CORINTHIANS 10:13 NLV

"Keep watch and pray, so that you will not give in to
temptation. For the spirit is willing, but the body is weak!"
MATTHEW 26:41 NLT

*Thank You, Lord, that You understand. Keep reminding me
that You were in all ways tempted just like I am, yet without
sin. It's so comforting to know that You have walked
this same path and were victorious. Amen.*

Truth

*It is truth that frees us, one that looms larger
than all the lies presently surrounding us.*
LISA BEVERE

And for their sakes I sanctify myself,
that they also might be sanctified through the truth.
JOHN 17:19 KJV

"Then you will know the truth, and the truth will set you free."
JOHN 8:32 NIV

Get the truth and never sell it; also get wisdom,
discipline, and good judgment.
PROVERBS 23:23 NLT

"He is the Spirit of Truth. The world cannot receive Him.
It does not see Him or know Him. You know Him
because He lives with you and will be in you."

JOHN 14:17 NLV

Finally, brethren, whatsoever things are true, whatsoever things are honest, whatsoever things are just, whatsoever things are pure, whatsoever things are lovely, whatsoever things are of good report; if there be any virtue, and if there be any praise, think on these things.

PHILIPPIANS 4:8 KJV

For the law was given through Moses; grace and truth came through Jesus Christ.

JOHN 1:17 NIV

For the Lord is good; his mercy is everlasting; and his truth endureth to all generations.

PSALM 100:5 KJV

For the word of the LORD holds true, and we can trust everything he does.

PSALM 33:4 NLT

God is a Spirit: and they that worship him must worship him in spirit and in truth.

JOHN 4:24 KJV

He is the Rock, his work is perfect: for all his ways
are judgment: a God of truth and without
iniquity, just and right is he.
DEUTERONOMY 32:4 KJV

Jesus said, "I am the Way and the Truth and the Life.
No one can go to the Father except by Me."
JOHN 14:6 NLV

Anyone who has good things come to him in the land
will have good things come to him by the God of truth.
And he who makes a promise in the land will
promise by the God of truth.
ISAIAH 65:16 NLV

These are the things you are to do: Speak the truth to each
other, and render true and sound judgment in your courts.
ZECHARIAH 8:16 NIV

*Father, You are the Source of truth. Teach me what is
true concerning You, and give me the courage to seek the
truth about myself. I am thankful that truth will triumph,
and that the followers of truth will be victorious. Amen.*

Understanding

Yearn to understand first and to be understood second.
BECA LEWIS ALLEN

And unto man he said, Behold, the fear of the LORD,
that is wisdom; and to depart from evil is understanding.
JOB 28:28 KJV

However, as it is written: "What no eye has seen, what no ear
has heard, and what no human mind has conceived"—the
things God has prepared for those who love him—these are
the things God has revealed to us by his Spirit. The Spirit
searches all things, even the deep things of God. For who
knows a person's thoughts except their own spirit
within them? In the same way no one knows the
thoughts of God except the Spirit of God.
1 CORINTHIANS 2:9–11 NIV

"But let him who speaks with pride speak about this, that he
understands and knows Me, that I am the Lord who shows
loving-kindness and does what is fair and right and good
on earth. For I find joy in these things," says the Lord.
JEREMIAH 9:24 NLV

Evil people don't understand justice, but those who
follow the Lord understand completely.
PROVERBS 28:5 NLT

Folly is joy to him that is destitute of wisdom:
but a man of understanding walketh uprightly.
PROVERBS 15:21 KJV

To one there is given through the Spirit a message
of wisdom, to another a message of knowledge
by means of the same Spirit.
1 CORINTHIANS 12:8 NIV

Joyful is the person who finds wisdom, the one who gains
understanding. For wisdom is more profitable than silver,
and her wages are better than gold. Wisdom is more
precious than rubies; nothing you desire
can compare with her.
PROVERBS 3:13–15 NLT

Are you strong because you belong to Christ? Does His love comfort you? Do you have joy by being as one in sharing the Holy Spirit? Do you have loving-kindness and pity for each other? Then give me true joy by thinking the same thoughts. Keep having the same love. Be as one in thoughts and actions.

PHILIPPIANS 2:1–2 NLV

In the lips of him that hath understanding wisdom is found: but a rod is for the back of him that is void of understanding.

PROVERBS 10:13 KJV

Cause me to understand the way of your precepts, that I may meditate on your wonderful deeds.

PSALM 119:27 NIV

I believe in your commands; now teach me good judgment and knowledge.

PSALM 119:66 NLT

The mind of him who has understanding looks for much learning, but the mouth of fools feeds on foolish ways.

PROVERBS 15:14 NLV

The heart of the prudent getteth knowledge;
and the ear of the wise seeketh knowledge.

PROVERBS 18:15 KJV

The rich are wise in their own eyes; one who is poor
and discerning sees how deluded they are.

PROVERBS 28:11 NIV

The tongue of the wise uses much learning in a good way,
but the mouth of fools speaks in a foolish way.

PROVERBS 15:2 NLV

Then you will understand what it means to fear
the LORD, and you will gain knowledge of God.
For the LORD grants wisdom! From his mouth
come knowledge and understanding.

PROVERBS 2:5–6 NLT

When I was a child, I spake as a child, I understood as
a child, I thought as a child: but when I became
a man, I put away childish things.
1 CORINTHIANS 13:11 KJV

For wisdom will enter your heart, and knowledge will
be pleasant to your soul. Discretion will protect you,
and understanding will guard you. Wisdom will save
you from the ways of wicked men, from men
whose words are perverse.
PROVERBS 2:10–12 NIV

Wisdom rests in the heart of one who has understanding,
but what is in the heart of fools is made known.
PROVERBS 14:33 NLV

"Wisdom belongs to the aged, and understanding to the
old. But true wisdom and power are found in God;
counsel and understanding are his."
JOB 12:12–13 NLT

*Lord, I often feel misunderstood. But thank You for
understanding me. Help me to turn to You, accepting
Your will for my life. When I can't understand
Your plan, help me to trust in You. Amen.*

Wisdom

*Intelligence is a measurement of things you know.
Wisdom is your ability to discern right from wrong and
make moral choices. A wise person will follow God.*
SONYA HASKINS

The wise heart will know the proper time and procedure.
ECCLESIASTES 8:5 NIV

Be wise now therefore, O ye kings:
be instructed, ye judges of the earth.
PSALM 2:10 KJV

Love wisdom like a sister; make insight a
beloved member of your family.
PROVERBS 7:4 NLT

Do not be foolish.
Understand what the Lord wants you to do.
EPHESIANS 5:17 NLV

185

Therefore whosoever heareth these sayings of mine,
and doeth them, I will liken him unto a wise man,
which built his house upon a rock: And the rain
descended, and the floods came, and the winds blew,
and beat upon that house; and it fell not:
for it was founded upon a rock.
MATTHEW 7:24–25 KJV

Whoever derides their neighbor has no sense,
but the one who has understanding holds their tongue.
PROVERBS 11:12 NIV

A prudent person foresees danger and takes
precautions. The simpleton goes blindly
on and suffers the consequences.
PROVERBS 22:3 NLT

"I, wisdom, live with understanding,
and I find much learning and careful thinking."
PROVERBS 8:12 NLV

The Lord by wisdom hath founded the earth;
by understanding hath he established the heavens.
By his knowledge the depths are broken up, and the
clouds drop down the dew. My son, let not them depart
from thine eyes: keep sound wisdom and discretion.

PROVERBS 3:19–21 KJV

The prudent keep their knowledge to themselves,
but a fool's heart blurts out folly.

PROVERBS 12:23 NIV

Those who listen to instruction will prosper; those who
trust the Lord will be joyful. The wise are known for their
understanding, and pleasant words are persuasive.

PROVERBS 16:20–21 NLT

Whoever is wise, let him understand these things and
know them. For the ways of the Lord are right,
and those who are right and good will follow
them, but sinners will not follow them.

HOSEA 14:9 NLV

My son, attend to my words; incline thine ear unto
my sayings. Let them not depart from thine eyes;
keep them in the midst of thine heart. For they are life
unto those that find them, and health to all their flesh.
PROVERBS 4:20–22 KJV

The teaching of the wise is a fountain of life, turning a
person from the snares of death. Good judgment wins favor,
but the way of the unfaithful leads to their destruction.
PROVERBS 13:14–15 NIV

Everyone knows that you are obedient to the Lord.
This makes me very happy. I want you to be wise
in doing right and to stay innocent of any wrong.
ROMANS 16:19 NLT

Those who are wise will shine like the bright heavens.
And those who lead many to do what is right and
good will shine like the stars forever and ever.

DANIEL 12:3 NLV

How much better is it to get wisdom than gold! and to get
understanding rather to be chosen than silver!
PROVERBS 16:16 KJV

Eat honey, my son, for it is good; honey from the comb is
sweet to your taste. Know also that wisdom is like honey
for you: If you find it, there is a future hope for
you, and your hope will not be cut off.
PROVERBS 24:13–14 NIV

In that day he will be your sure foundation, providing a
rich store of salvation, wisdom, and knowledge.
The fear of the LORD will be your treasure.
ISAIAH 33:6 NLT

I will show you and teach you in the way you should go.
I will tell you what to do with My eye upon you.

PSALM 32:8 NLV

If any of you lack wisdom, let him ask of God, that giveth to all
men liberally, and upbraideth not; and it shall be given him.

JAMES 1:5 KJV

We do, however, speak a message of wisdom among the
mature, but not the wisdom of this age or of the rulers of
this age, who are coming to nothing. No, we declare God's
wisdom, a mystery that has been hidden and that God
destined for our glory before time began. None of
the rulers of this age understood it, for if they had,
they would not have crucified the Lord of glory.

1 CORINTHIANS 2:6–8 NIV

Those who are wise will take all this to heart;
they will see in our history the faithful love of the LORD.

PSALM 107:43 NLT

The person who thinks he knows all
the answers still has a lot to learn.
1 Corinthians 8:2 nlv

A good man sheweth favour, and lendeth:
he will guide his affairs with discretion.
Psalm 112:5 kjv

Wisdom is a shelter as money is a shelter, but the advantage
of knowledge is this: Wisdom preserves those who have it.
Ecclesiastes 7:12 niv

*Lord Jesus, You have promised that if I ask for wisdom,
You will give it to me. I ask for a sharp mind and
sound judgment to be used for Your glory. Amen.*